Without Help or Hindrance

Without Help or Hindrance

Religious Identity in American Culture

By
ELDON G. ERNST

THE WESTMINSTER PRESS
Philadelphia

Copyright © 1977 The Westminster Press

BOOK DESIGN BY DOROTHY ALDEN SMITH

Published by The Westminster Press®
Philadelphia, Pennsylvania

PRINTED IN THE UNITED STATES OF AMERICA

Library of Congress Cataloging in Publication Data

Ernst, Eldon G
    Without help or hindrance.

    Bibliography: p.
    Includes index.
    1. Christianity—United States. I. Title.
BR515.E76   209'.73   76-27742
ISBN 0-664-24128-X

To
Bydell and Kenneth
Daisy and John
Loving Parents All

Contents

Preface

This book celebrates the religious pluralism that has flourished in America over the past two hundred years. It also recognizes the problems that confront Christians struggling with their identity in this religiously pluralistic society.

My immediate purpose is to set the problem of Christian identity in the context of American religious history. My long-range goal is to help modern American Christians to understand better who they have been, who they now are, and who they might become.

I have portrayed the historical development of Christianity in America primarily for nonspecialist readers. These readers will find that the problem of Christian identity remains unsolved in this book. But the book will have reached its goal if it helps to clarify the problem which only American Christians can solve for themselves in their many ways.

Readers who are acquainted with the main currents in the writing of American religious history of the past several decades will recognize the influence of prominent scholars on my thinking. The bibliographic essay at the end of the book gives a few of the better-known works of some of these scholars.

The context within which this book emerged has been broadly ecumenical. The substance and structure of the book was developed in the give-and-take with ministers, laypersons, students, and scholars in conjunction with lectures that I presented from 1974 to 1976. These were given in different forms at the Pacific School of Religion Pastoral Conference in Berkeley, the World Mission Conference at Asilomar in Pacific Grove, California, and the Lay School of Theology in Medford, Oregon.

Over a longer period my ideas have taken form while I was working with students in the Graduate Theological Union in Berkeley. These students were preparing for leadership roles in America's many religious communities, and some have become leaders in Europe, Asia, Africa, and South America. They have ingrained in me a universal bias. Truth comes to humankind from many sources. Unlimited growth and creativity take place when diverse persons struggle, study, argue, and celebrate with one another in the areas of their deepest convictions, concerns, and questions.

Finally, I wish to acknowledge my immediate colleagues who in many ways have helped provide an environment within which study and research can happen: Paul D. Clasper, Harold B. Frazee, William R. Herzog, II, Robert B. Laurin, William L. Malcomson, and Ida J. Thornton.

E.G.E.

Berkeley, California

Introduction

What does it mean to be identified as a Christian in America? Are Christians to be thought of as superior citizens whose religious faith harmonizes with the essential nature and destiny of the nation? Or does Christianity conflict with the basic character of American life, thought, and institutions? Apart from these two extremes, what possible relationships are there, if any, between one's religion and one's national citizenship?

For many Christians today who are struggling with their sense of religious identity, these are vital questions. Our nation, now two hundred years old, seems riddled with disease. The churches appear to be dying of old age. Some traditional assumptions about the nature and destiny of Christianity and America have been crumbling.

Yet the situation is not entirely new. Similar questions confronted the churches when the American nation was born. Then, as now, Christian identity in America seemed highly complex and deeply problematic.

The United States began as a nation without a state religion. Cultural inheritance, however, identified Americans with Christendom. Histori-

11

cally "Christendom" refers to those societies, especially European, in which Christianity was the official or privileged religion. The Christian church was the dominant, often exclusive, religious institution permeating all aspects of culture. Eighteenth-century Americans related both positively and negatively to European Christendom which for centuries had defined Western civilization. Some Americans believed that their nation was called to be the instrument of Christian victory throughout the world. Others celebrated their nation's triumph over the ecclesiastical powers associated with Christendom.

However varied their hopes and expectations, most of the first generation of American Christians recognized that conditions in the new nation would challenge the very existence of organized Christianity.

During the quarter century surrounding the American Revolution, church life plunged to an all-time low, with few apparent signs of recovery. The social upheaval connected with war had disrupted many congregations. Efforts normally devoted to religious matters were given over to the social and political problems of organizing a new nation. European and colonial American state church ties were broken and traditional parish structures upset. The large majority of the people were out of touch with organized Christianity. Those who remained active in church life had to face the fact that to be an American citizen and to be a Christian did not necessarily go hand in hand. At best the two would have to learn how to live together out of wedlock.

The problem was aggravated by those who forecast the end of organized Christianity as a significant element in the new society. Radical advocates of free thought pronounced traditional church practices and beliefs outmoded for a nation born in the age and spirit of enlightenment. In the judgment of these eighteenth-century rationalists, the Christian churches contained decaying remnants of medieval society. They should be sentenced to obscurity as sects irrelevant to modern public life —there finally to die.

Church leaders recognized their predicament. Confronted by social disorder and radical ideologies, how could they maintain their identity as Christians? In a free society with no ordered place for the church, what could be the Christians' role? The violence of the French Revolution after 1789 appeared to have overthrown all semblance of Christian civilization in that part of Europe. This increased the American Christians' uncertainty of the future. Christendom might be doomed in the Old World. Could it survive in the New?

The mere survival of European-fashioned Christianity in America would not suffice. In a developing free society expanding over a vast geographical frontier, much of traditional church life would be impossible to perpetuate. Christianity in America would assume novel forms. In fact, innovation would carry the day. In this context Christians would seek their identity outside the boundaries of Old World Christendom. They were New World Christians, Americans on the frontier of Western civilization.

How Christians in America have understood

and expressed their identity over the past two hundred years is the subject of this book.

Never has there been one proper way to be Christian in America. From the beginning a variety of Christian orientations have flourished. Today it is apparent that there is no one way to identify oneself as a Christian in America. In this nation without *a church* there are *many churches;* indeed, there are many religions. The story develops a theme of unfolding pluralism.[1]

The book is organized according to my understanding of the various ways in which Christians have responded to the American environment of religious freedom and the separation of church and state. There are two underlying themes. One is the tension between private and public dimensions of religion. The other is the challenge made to any particular belief system by the conflicting truth claims of many different religious persuasions. These two themes are interrelated. They are woven into the different patterns of Christian identity in America.

The first three chapters describe several of these patterns. Here we are concerned especially with persons and groups that have concentrated on the distinctive characteristics of their particular religious tradition. These include experience, doctrine, moral-ethical discipline, and style of communal organization. For various reasons they have developed their Christian identity according to how they differed religiously from others and how they separated themselves from the dominant characteristics of American life and thought. By choice or by necessity they have nurtured the private more than the public expression of their religion. They have been aware of themselves as religious minorities, free to express their own faith as they saw fit, but quite distinguishable from the main currents of popular and public life in America.

Consequently these Christians usually have projected an exclusive image in their communities. Often they have thought of themselves primarily as a special people who bear the Christian way uniquely within society-at-large. Some have maintained their Christian individuality through separation from public life. Others have identified themselves actively as public citizens in every aspect of their lives except the religious. As Christians they gathered out of the world for worship and fellowship among their own, keeping religion "in its private place." At times such Christians have become publicly visible as nonconformists, or advocates of some "righteous" cause. Their dissenting activities have sharpened the distinctive characteristics of their religious life and thought.

Chapter 4 explores a different kind of Christian identity in America. Here we trace the integration of Christianity into the social order through the public involvement and influence of Christian individuals and churches. Churches of this type have jockeyed for position as the nation's recognized major Christian denominations. Among them the Methodists, Baptists, Presbyterians, Congregationalists, Unitarians, Episcopalians, and eventually Lutherans and Roman Catholics have enjoyed dominant positions. Others have had similar aspirations. Within these churches Christians have identified themselves as bearers of the nation's majority religious force. The private and public expressions of their religious faith have blended well with the most popular and widespread customs, ideology, and institutions of American culture.

These public-oriented Christians have envisaged a Christian America. Bearing the imprint of European Christendom, they have assumed that the church should permeate all of public as well as private life. This inspired them to undertake the task of molding their nation into a Christian civilization.

In a Christian civilization the churches and society would be thoroughly interrelated. Ideally the church would include everyone. Persons would be identified as Christian by heritage, custom, and cultural osmosis. Consequently American Christians with this outlook have tended to emphasize the inclusive nature of their churches. Nominal participants along with the "pillars" of the church have been welcomed as full members. They have been able to differ widely in theology and forms of worship without breaking their deeper sense of unity. Different denominational traditions generally have acknowledged one another as valid expressions of the Christian church. Members have been religiously mobile, moving from church to church without strict regard for denominational affiliation. "After all," they have reasoned, "when you get right down to it most churches teach pretty much the same thing." Their common sense of identity as Christian Americans, in the final analysis, has more than balanced their separate associations with particular church traditions or denominations.

These, then, are two different religious orientations in America—two frameworks within which Christians have constructed their religious identities. One developed into a minority awareness, a concentration on religious distinctiveness, and a basically private-oriented expression of religion. The other developed into a majority consciousness, an emphasis on the unity undergirding diverse religious traditions, and a public-oriented expression of religion.

To be sure, we exaggerate simplistically when we divide the many kinds of American Christians into two large categories. Some qualification is in order.[2]

Usually the two orientations have overlapped and mixed together. Few Christians have fully isolated their religion from their participation in and identification with the American society-at-large. Fewer still have failed totally to distinguish their religious faith and the distinctive characteristics of their particular religious tradition from their American loyalties and national consciousness.

Most denominations have held fast to their conviction that they embody the superior expression of Christianity. In part this is what has held them together as identifiable traditions. At the same time, most minority-conscious Christian communities have maintained some sense of commonality with Christians other than themselves. Few have been absolutely exclusive, and most would gladly experience wide representation and influence in society.

Furthermore, small exclusive groups of Christians at times have become publicly visible and influential. In some instances large inclusive groups have restricted themselves to the private sector. Public Christians have not necessarily been the most creative Christian voices in society, for often they simply have embraced the *status quo,* assuming that society already was essentially Christian in nature. In most churches, whatever their basic orientation toward other Christians and the American social order, the private and the public elements of religion have coexisted.

Nevertheless, as the chapters that follow will show, Christians in America have leaned toward one or the other of these two basic religious orientations in expressing their sense of identity. Indeed, nothing has divided Christians more sharply than their opinions about how, if at all, organized religion should be involved in public issues.

In the final chapter we shall discover that the religious situation in twentieth-century America has made the problem of Christian identity even more complicated. The majority-minority, inclusive-exclusive, and public-private tensions in American religious life are taking on new forms and moving in new directions. The search for identity has become critical.

In a free society all religions are equal before the law. This is the fundamental public meaning of religious freedom. The private meaning allows individuals and groups to worship and act according to their persuasions in faith, limited only with respect to the equal religious freedom of others. Hence public and private religious freedom are intertwined.

In this environment the American family of religions has become large and diverse. The unique integrity of each person and group finds endless expressions within the common national community. If Christian identity in this kind of nation is complex for Americans of the present generation, they can look over the past two hundred years for some precedents as to why it is so. They may also find clues to assist them in their quest for identity.

1

The American Religious Revolution: New Freedoms, New Americans, New Churches

The American Revolution reached one of its more radical settlements on November 3, 1791. On that day the First Amendment to the Federal Constitution went into effect. It read, in part, as follows:

Congress shall make no law respecting an establishment of religion, or prohibiting the free exercise thereof.

Church and state were legally separated, placing all religious organizations on an equal status in the civil order. Religious freedom became the law of the land. The government and the people should be free from religious coercion, and the churches should be free from state control. From now on, relationships between organized religion and civil institutions should be on a nonsectarian basis, allowing no privilege to some churches over others, and respecting the religious rights of all citizens.

A religious revolution had taken place.

RELIGIOUS FREEDOM

It may be difficult for us, two hundred years later, to understand the significance of this event. For over fourteen hundred years the Western world had assumed that a stable social order depended upon all people belonging to one church. Not to enforce uniformity would lead to anarchy. Since there was but one true faith, there could be only one true church. Although their roles were distinct, the church and the state worked together, in mutual support, to sustain a solid religious foundation for a unified society. This was Christendom: civilization centered in the Christian church.

Christendom exploded in the sixteenth century. The Protestant Reformation and the Roman Catholic "counter reforms" broke apart the outward unity of the church. This set the stage for the modern drama of Christian pluralism.

Few persons in the sixteenth century fully understood what had happened. They could not imagine toleration, much less public freedom and equality, of several different church traditions within a single body politic. Even as European and British explorers were extending their Old World empires into the New World, their nations were adjusting to the shattered Christendom by establishing one church or another as the official religion of their respective states. New Spain and New France enforced religious uniformity. Most of the early settlers of New England likewise expected that it would be necessary to enforce religious uniformity here.

In the British colonies, however, religious uniformity soon became an impossibility. Here the

ruptures within Christendom led to a more radical
kind of religious arrangement. Some of the colonies did attempt to enforce uniformity through
tax-supported churches and by punishing dissenters. The Anglican (Episcopal) Church was established in parts of the South; the Congregational
Church was established in several New England
colonies. Other churches survived these situations
as nonconformists, sometimes at the cost of persecution. Yet some nonconformist groups eventually
thrived as popular alternatives to the standing order churches.

There simply was no holding back the forces
that religious uniformity encountered. Persons of
many religious persuasions streamed out of the
Old World parishes, crossed the Atlantic Ocean,
and settled into the New World towns and wilderness. Devout believers, nominal Christians, and
the unchurched formed a mixed population. Old
World religious structures and customs were challenged by New World environment and experiences. The situation invited the growth of diverse
religious movements, experiments, and organizations.

Consequently by the end of the seventeenth
century the British colonies in America contained
most of the varieties of Christianity that had
emerged in England and Europe. Some took on
characteristics peculiar to their new environment.
One historian has caught the flavor of the mixture
especially well:

> A traveler in 1700 making his way from Boston to
> the Carolinas would encounter Congregationalists
> of varying intensity, Baptists of several varieties,

Presbyterians, Quakers, and several other forms of Puritan radicalism; Dutch, German, and French Reformed; Swedish, Finnish, and German Lutherans; Mennonites and radical pietists, Anglicans, Roman Catholics; here and there a Jewish congregation, a few Rosicrucians; and, of course, a vast number of the unchurched—some of them powerfully alienated from any form of institutional religion.[1]

During the decades that followed, as the American Revolution approached, religious pluralism kept apace with the growing population. A difficult task lay ahead for those persons responsible for drawing up state and federal constitutions for the new Republic. Most everyone acknowledged the importance of religion in society. But how could a people so diversified religiously be brought together into a united civil order? There was no real precedent to follow in arriving at a religious settlement in America.

Some argued that, as in England, the government should support one church throughout the country, while allowing other churches to exist by their own support. This would guarantee a consistent religious tradition as a unifying force within the society. But again, how could a people whose religious loyalties were so mixed reach agreement on a single state church? Any church chosen would provide a focus of identity for only a small minority of the nation's Christian citizens. As a source of religious unity it would be a straw church.

Others argued, therefore, that the Federal Government should honor whatever churches the individual states might elect to establish within their own borders. But this would create a plurality of official national churches, which would be counterproductive to national unity and lead to unreasonable complexity. Moreover, how would the states decide which churches to favor?

Would it be possible to make Christianity-in-general the official religion in America? Tax monies could be directed to all kinds of Christian churches. But who could define Christianity to the satisfaction of all who claimed the faith? Some Christians did not even recognize the identity of other Christians. The government would spark endless conflicts trying to decide which churches were to be considered Christian and therefore worthy of financial support.

Clearly, the only reasonable conclusion was not to have an established state religion at all. On no other grounds could the states accept a federal constitution. The constitution would have to guarantee the rights of persons to go their own ways with regard to religion, including the right to reject religion in any form without fear of suffering discrimination. Religious organizations, being essentially private, could become involved in public life only by their own initiative. Without civil authority, churches could wield power in society only through means of popular persuasion. As a public force, organized religion always would have to submit to the private religious rights of citizens and churches. Though twisted at times for particular religious interests, and sometimes disobeyed, this would become the nation's law regarding religion.

In other words, religious pluralism made religious freedom necessary. The inherited idea that a society could be unified only through one common church gave way to the revolutionary conclusion that this new society could find unity only through the disestablishment of all churches.

There were other reasons why church leaders as well as political leaders supported the separation of church and state in America. Persons who had suffered social and economic discrimination for their nonconforming religious practices naturally leaned toward full religious freedom in the nation. They had everything to gain and nothing to lose. Among these were Baptists, Quakers, Roman Catholics, Presbyterians, and other groups who appeared threatening enough to the established churches to evoke some form of persecution. Religious coercion nurtured the desire for religious freedom.

Furthermore, the fact that nonconforming churches could prosper on their own support led many to believe in the spiritual benefits of religious freedom. The Great Awakening (an enthusiastic revival of religion throughout the colonies) of the 1730's and 1740's helped prove this point, especially to the Baptists. The revival preachers sparked new enthusiasm among persons with no church affiliation as well as among active church members. Newly converted believers disregarded traditionally accepted patterns of religious behavior and brought vitality into church life.

Many converts joined Baptist churches, which were not encumbered by entanglements with civil government. Baptist sympathies lay with nonconformity. The practices of believer's baptism made sense to persons convinced that the life of the church depended upon the experienced faith of its members. Converts joined and supported the churches solely on the strength of their convictions. This distinguished them from members of state churches who were baptized into the church as newborn infants and who associated with churches as a matter of custom and habit. In some cases this meant supporting two churches, one voluntarily and the other (state church) by enforced taxation. Yet the voluntarily supported Baptist churches grew by leaps and bounds during the later 1700's, while the state churches waned.

Many Christians simply had come to believe that religious faith by its very nature must be free. Coercion and belief were incompatible. The writings of earlier opponents of enforced religious uniformity such as Roger Williams (*The Bloody Tenent of Persecution,* 1644) and William Penn (*The Great Case of Liberty of Conscience,* 1670) had made their impact. Freedom of conscience was the way to truth. Of course they defined truth narrowly in the eighteenth-century evangelical and pietistic sense. Truth was personal, spiritual knowledge of Christ leading to a righteous moral life. Yet religious freedom became the logical conclusion of this line of thought. The Baptist preacher Isaac Backus thus could include in his famous tract on religious liberty (1778) the idea that "true religion is a voluntary obedience unto God."[2]

Church leaders like Backus provided support to the framers of the Constitution who presented similar arguments for religious freedom, though from different theological outlooks. Some of the most influential political theorists of the new nation were deists, steeped in the tolerant ideas of the age of reason. Their influence on American thought went far beyond their numbers. Deists embraced a kind of natural religion in which God's universal laws were known to humankind through reason and observation of the created world. To their mind the various dogmas and rituals that characterized and divided the churches were extra baggage which hindered more than helped one's true religious understanding. The churches' claims to special revelation were misleading. Natural revelation, given to all persons, was sufficient—there was no other kind. Reasonable persons, whatever their church membership (or lack of it), could agree on the *essential* principles of faith: God exists; God should be worshiped; true worship is the practice of virtue; wrongdoing requires repentance; and rewards and punishments come after death.

Now deists, like most of their contemporaries, assumed that commonly shared religious beliefs helped hold a society together. But they also were convinced that religious truths were bound to no church. Indeed, it was clear that the commonly held beliefs of the American people, as well as their various "nonessential" dogmas, were spread out among the many different churches. Therefore no particular church should be allowed to dominate the people's minds against their wills. Yet neither should churches be squelched, for they provided the framework within which many people freely worshiped God and cultivated virtuous

lives. The essentials of true faith shared by all
thoughtful persons, which might unite the new
Republic, could be lived within as well as outside
the churches.

The important point was that free worship is the
only true worship. Here deists agreed with orthodox churchmen, though they might be worlds
apart theologically. James Madison, later to become the fourth President of the United States,
argued in his powerful "Memorial and Remonstrance" before the Virginia General Assembly of
1786 with words much like Backus', quoted above.
Religion, wrote Madison, "can be directed only by
reason and conviction, not by force or violence.
The religion of every man must be left to the conviction and conscience of every man; and it is the
right of every man to exercise it as these may dic-
tate."[3]

Truth breaks through and God is known to the
free mind and the willing heart. Persons who differed theologically could share this conviction, and
religious liberty became their logical conclusion.
Men like Benjamin Franklin, John Adams, James
Madison, and Thomas Jefferson argued for the separation of church and state in theory as well as
from the practical necessity to respect the religious pluralism that already existed in America.
They became the natural political leaders of those
who had labored unwillingly under state churches
and had suffered for their beliefs.

It is important to understand that arguments for
the separation of church and state in the interest
of the free conscience of the individual did not
necessarily lead to mere individualism. Religiously

free persons and churches could apply their faith and traditions to the civil order. Evangelical churchmen and deists alike expected religion to contribute to the formation of responsible citizens and stable social institutions.

The First Amendment to the Constitution therefore recognized the private rights of persons and groups in religious matters. Their public religious rights followed suit, for among private rights was the right to participate in public life. Simple enough! But what may seem like a simple, clearcut religious settlement in America has proved to be most complex. Throughout American history private religious interests often have clashed with the public civil order in ways unforeseen by those who legislated the First Amendment.[4]

The American religious revolution reached completion as state governments followed the pattern set by the Federal Constitution. (Massachusetts was the last to abolish its state church, in 1838.) The implications of this revolution were to be far-reaching, presenting challenges and opportunities beyond the wildest imagination of eighteenth-century Americans.

It was clear immediately that churches previously supported by taxes now would have to survive on their own in free competition with other religious groups. Historic prestige and privilege enjoyed by certain churches no longer would carry much weight. Church authority could function only by its power of persuasion over those choosing to acquiesce. Church teachings, practices, and methods that were directly relevant to people's felt needs might wield the greatest power.

Soon the promotion of religion would become a major concern of church leaders. Success would come to those who could adjust church structures to a people on the move in a vast geographical span and who could bring religion to bear on loosely organized, at times lawless, and often lonely social situations. Religious freedom would open the field for those persons and groups with religious incentive and imagination.

As the nineteenth century unfolded in the context of this experiment in religious liberty, a maze of diverse religious forms and activities began to emerge. An ever-changing, ever-moving population became a significant factor in this process. Through immigration the world's rich variety of religious life continually poured into America. As this happened, the problem of Christian identity became increasingly complicated, especially for the immigrants.

UNCEASING RELIGIOUS IMMIGRATION

Religion in America offers variety to match the peoples of the world. Most of it originally was imported by immigrants who never ceased arriving. Then began the process of "Americanization," which brought new diversity as well as commonality to American religious life.

Immigrants noticeably began to affect the religious makeup of the nation early in the nineteenth century. Protestants and Roman Catholics from western and northern Europe brought their deeply ingrained traditions into the United States.

Here they clashed with, adjusted to, and finally altered what were becoming peculiarly American religious characteristics.

Such words as "novelty," "ultraism," "voluntaryism," and "pluralism" consistently have been used to describe religion in America. Eventually "pragmatism" would characterize religion as thoroughly American. (We shall return to these characteristics in the chapters that follow).

Often American religious life took the form of "movements" out of which new churches and other organizations emerged. These new movements resulted from many traditions struggling to grow in the American environment of competitive religious free enterprise. People had to take hold of their freedom, become self-sufficient, and use their imaginations and talents aggressively and cleverly in relating religion to new circumstances. Churches that were inclined to maintain their traditions soon found it necessary to adjust them to people's needs and desires.

In this way a variety of Old World traditions accommodated afresh with each new wave of immigrants. Most such accommodation further divided the people, whose willingness to change their ways was not consistent. The result was an ever-widening range of religious pluralism.

The newcomers settled everywhere—in urban and rural areas, in more established Eastern cities as well as all over the Western frontier. They mingled with one another and among the older "native-born" citizens. Even immigrants of Christian traditions already represented in America frequently were cast into the mold of foreigners ripe for Americanization. Segregation, partly forced upon them and often chosen by them, became the context out of which these people were assimilated into the nation without totally losing their sense of identity. To a remarkable extent immigrants established relatively separate communities of their own, scattering throughout the country "hyphenated-American" towns, communities, neighborhoods, and above all churches.

The process of immigration continued throughout the nineteenth century, picking up steam especially late in the century and early in the twentieth century. Not only did the numbers of immigrants increase but the extent of pluralism widened as peoples came from diverse places. A brief look at some statistics will tell the story.

During the one hundred and fifty years between 1820 and 1970 approximately forty-five million people entered the United States.[5] The greatest thrust came between 1880 and 1930, when approximately twenty-eight million arrived. The peak was reached during the first decade of the twentieth century, when nearly nine million people came to America (just under a million each year). Therefore we might expect that in 1930 about one fourth of the entire United States population were first- or second-generation immigrants.

Of the forty-five million immigrants that arrived between 1820 and 1970 about thirty-five million came from Europe; over seven million came from other parts of the Americas; one and a half million came from Asia. They joined an already mixed population of European-Americans, Afro-Americans, and native Indian-Americans.

The great influx that arrived after 1880 became known as the "new immigration" because so many of them came from southern and eastern Europe. They were Protestants, Roman Catholics, Jews, and Eastern Orthodox Christians of backgrounds quite different from the majority of Americans. Despite the restrictive immigration laws of the 1920's, people have continued to come from many parts of the world. In recent years the migration of peoples from Spanish-speaking countries in Central and South America and from the Caribbean Islands has again altered the religious makeup of America.

As immigrants arrived in America they were presented with national ideals and values to which their religious communities helped them adjust. They were promised a new life, a new beginning of equal opportunity in a land of plenty. But they also were promised freedom to be themselves, freedom to maintain their cultural heritage which included, above all, their religion. They felt the tension in these twin promises of the American way—to be able to hold on to inherited personal identification with the old country while starting over in a new place with its own national identity. For "hyphenated-Americans" the religious community often provided the cultural base within which to retain enough of their old customs and beliefs to feel secure, self-confident, and at home in the new land.

Churches became facilitators of transition from the old to the new. They became a refuge from total newness, yet they were part of American society. They were therefore a key factor in the assimilation process. But assimilation was not so much a "melting pot" as an endless process of particular communities developing within society-at-large. Immigrant churches presented a context of meaning which, though related to American promises and expectations, was not bound to them.

Disappointment came to new Americans when equality of opportunity was countered by prejudice and discrimination. No matter how hard they worked, there were obstacles in their way to success. Because of their strange language accents and unfamiliar cultural habits, their loyalty to the nation was questioned no matter how avidly they obeyed the laws and expressed their patriotism. Their loneliness, due to separation from their friends and relatives who remained in the old country, made life in the new country miserable. Even social and economic advancement did not fulfill their lives completely in the new world.

It would be natural for immigrants, failing to attain their fondest personal hopes in the American promised land, to project those hopes onto the nation itself. They could find some satisfaction in the nation's growing power and prosperity. They might find solace in identifying with American democratic ideals and institutions and in sheer national pride. Small wonder that new Americans, promised more than they could achieve yet receiving more than they had left behind, often became the nation's superpatriots.

Yet more often than not their churches offered something more consistently rewarding than did their new nationalism. As American citizens they remained public foreigners—they were "different" from native-born Americans who controlled public institutions and set the nation's dominant cultural patterns. But in their churches immigrants felt less like foreigners. There they could identify as Christian Americans at home in their particular traditions and cultural groupings. The extent to which immigrant churches provided a framework of identity which combined Old and New World citizenships while transcending both is apparent in the following quotation about German-Americans:

> The German immigrant naturally brought his prejudices with him to America as part of his cultural baggage. He sought out others of his own kind in this country, often relatives or acquaintances, persons who shared his own culture, language, and religion and who were most likely to give him the advice and assistance he needed to make a start in America. In this way concentrations of like-minded Germans developed—Catholics here, Lutherans there, and Mennonites and other sectarians somewhere else. Each group had surprisingly little to do with the other. Each went its own way, developing its religiously oriented social, educational, and sometimes economic and political institutions. The only common bond these groups of Germans had, other than general culture and language, was a commitment to religious values. They identified themselves first of all as Catholics, Lutherans, Evangelicals, Mennonites, or Methodists, and only secondarily (sometimes only incidently) as Germans. Most, of course, were keenly conscious of their German character and gave explicit expression to their hopes and goals

within that context. Yet when they perceived that being German obstructed or prevented the attainment of their goals as church people, the majority were prepared to cast off their ethnicity to whatever extent was possible or necessary. In short, they were *Kirchendeutschen*—"church Germans."[6]

RELIGIOUS INNOVATION, CONFLICT, AND DIVERSITY

Under the impact of religious freedom, imported churches were stretched, torn apart, and reshaped in America. People free to go their own ways religiously would not submit to churches that did not satisfy new needs and desires. Dissatisfied members were free to change the church if they could, or to leave it and start up a new one more to their liking. Hence American church history is a story of the endless splintering of churches, often for minute and seemingly insignificant reasons. It also is the story of the gradual Americanization of European church traditions.

Often divisiveness and change within the churches have come about through the clash of differing religious convictions and experiences, not to mention their struggles for power. Movements of reform and rejuvenation continually have divided churches and brought new ones into being. Often these new movements were responding to alterations in traditional theology as well as to a decline in religious enthusiasm and discipline in church life. In these situations it did not matter much whether the guardians of traditions or the innovators of new movements finally controlled the church; division came in either case.

This pattern had colonial roots. The eighteenth-century evangelical revivals produced "new lights" who distinguished themselves from "old lights." The new lights identified themselves according to their spiritual experiences, their theology, and their newly found dedication to a more "pure" form of worship and a more "virtuous" style of life. Such innovations as itinerate preaching, open-air services, greater lay involvement in corporate worship, and mystic-ecstatic expressions in public meetings separated them from the old lights. Even today evidence of this division may be seen in New Haven, Connecticut. On the New Haven Green two Congregational churches (now United Church of Christ) stand side by side. They are separate corporations with separate programs, direct descendants of the new and the old lights respectively.

Throughout American history, revivalism has divided as much as united Christian communities. Support and opposition cut across and through the denominations. First-generation immigrants and older Americans alike took both sides. Revivalism was controversial partly because it featured many American "departures" from European Christian traditions in areas of theology, worship, spiritual development, and community life. "Innovation" in religion became the key bone of contention as old religious traditions sought to come to terms with the American environment. The innovations projected in revivalism forced the issue.

The American environment itself challenged Christian traditions. Many competing churches in a society of religious freedom, a mobile population expanding across a vast geographical frontier and mixing together in growing cities, and the forces of democracy and individualism all rubbed hard against the controlling forces of inherited European church traditions. America was being experienced as an innovative society.

In this context Christians wondered which elements in their faith were absolute and unchangeable and which were open to change with new times and places. Of course they differed in their judgments. New England Unitarians and transcendentalists pondered "the transient and permanent in Christianity." On the frontier the Disciples of Christ decried innovations. They called for the restoration of primitive New Testament Christianity in the American free environment, hoping thereby to unite all Christians who had been divided by innovative traditions. In the process the Disciples of Christ became yet another new and innovative Protestant denomination born on American soil. Roman Catholics debated throughout the nineteenth century over the "accidents" and the "essentials" in Christianity. The accidents of the church's formation and practice were dependent upon a particular time and place. These could be changed and adjusted to the American environment. The essentials of the church could not be altered. But which were accidents and which were essentials? Which is transient and which is permanent?[7]

The most consistent and influential defenders of

innovation as part of the essential in Christianity
arose among the Methodists. Methodism became
an innovative force widely influential among Protestants outside the Methodist Church itself.
Charles G. Finney, though not specifically a Methodist, expressed the Methodist perspective clearly.
He frankly celebrated innovation as God's means
of church reform throughout church history. The
life of the spirit took priority over the forms of
theology and church practice characteristic of a
particular time and place. John Wesley's Methodist awakening within the Church of England during the eighteenth century represented an apparent modern outburst of spiritual reform whose
innovative forms brought it into conflict with the
Mother Church. The "new measures" which Finney introduced in revival meetings could, he
thought, be seen as the flowering of church reform
in the new American environment.

> If we examine the history of the church we shall
> find that there never has been an extensive refor-
> mation, except by new measures. . . . Perhaps it is
> not too much to say, that it is impossible for God
> himself to bring about reformations but by new
> measures. At least, it is a fact that God has *always
> chosen* this way, and the wisest and best that he
> could devise or adopt. And although it has always
> been the case, that the very measures which God
> has chosen to employ, and which he has blessed in
> reviving his work, have been opposed as new mea-
> sures, and have been denounced, yet he has con-
> tinued to act upon the same principle. When he
> has found that a certain mode has lost its influence
> by having become a form, he brings up some new

measure, which will *Break In* upon their lazy habits, and *Wake Up* a slumbering church. And great good has resulted.[8]

Those who denounced Finney's new measures defended tradition. They usually judged these innovations to be typical American "excesses" (ultraism) lacking the spiritual depth and historical continuity of mature Christianity. No one more forcefully argued against the revival system than did John Williamson Nevin, a nineteenth-century Scotch-Irish Presbyterian who taught successively at Princeton, Western Theological Seminary near Pittsburgh, and the German Reformed seminary at Mercersburg, Pennsylvania. Comparing revivalism to the traditional "system of the catechism," Nevin found revivalism wanting. According to him, revivalism was a superficial "whirlwind process" which produced "a sickly Christianity." He described "revival machinery" as "solemn tricks for effect, decision displays at the bidding of the preacher, genuflections and prostrations in the aisle or around the altar, noise and disorder, extravagance and rant, mechanical conversions, justification by feeling rather than faith, and encouragement ministered to all fanatical impressions."[9]

This kind of language fanned the fires of strife among Christians. Revivalism, though not unique to America, was one practical adaptation of Christianity to the American environment. It also assumed a distinctive force and expression in America. It stimulated social reforms. It brought together Christians of different traditions in a common religious experience. But it also was controversial and divisive. Some thought that much of Christianity was lost in revivalism, while others thought that much was gained. Although revivalism swept the nation throughout the nineteenth century and penetrated the large industrial cities at the turn of the century, it never ceased dividing the churches.

Within the context of revivalism, several distinctive Christian movements developed into major traditions built upon certain doctrines, experiences, and practice. Their concentration on certain areas of Christian life and thought, often at the expense of other areas, is partly what traditionalists have criticized as American religious "excesses." It is the sectarian tendency in American Christianity. Such excesses have existed throughout church history, but seldom have they thrived as freely as they have in America.

For example, the nineteenth-century Holiness movement, which emerged within Methodism and spread into other denominations, produced many new churches and denominations within the general Wesleyan tradition. The Wesleyan Methodist Church and the Free Methodist Church were mid-nineteenth-century Holiness secessions from mainline Methodism. The Christian and Missionary Alliance, the Church of the Nazarene, and the Salvation Army were but three later products of this widespread movement. They stressed the doctrine and inward experience of perfect sanctification through a "second blessing," the state of sinlessness beyond one's original conversion experience.

At the same time, late in the nineteenth century, various Churches of God developed out of a Pentecostal movement which was closely related to the Holiness revival. Pentecostalists practiced faith healing and focused on tongue-speaking and other outward displays of religious experience (a "third blessing" baptism of the Holy Spirit). The Assemblies of God and the Foursquare Gospel were among the Pentecostal churches that originated early in the twentieth century.

During the early twentieth century the Dispensationalist and Fundamentalist movements tore apart the Baptists, Presbyterians, and Disciples of Christ and produced new church bodies. They emphasized certain doctrinal positions, especially belief in Christ's unique divinity and supernatural atonement for human sin. They upheld a particular understanding of the "verbal inspiration" and "infallible literal truth" of the Bible and its absolute authority in all areas of Christian life and thought. Dispensationalists formulated a view of reality within which human history is preordained by God and centered in the premillennial "second coming" of Christ to earth. With this event all persons would be judged and Christ's thousand-year reign would begin. "Dispensations" are historical periods of new supernatural revelations in human history which these Christians find recorded and prophesied in the Bible.[10] The Seventh-day Adventists and the Jehovah's Witnesses are two of the most vigorous new churches that developed out of the general premillennial movement.

By 1960 the combined membership of the Holiness, Pentecostal, and Fundamentalist and Dispensationalist groups was nearly 8,500,000 persons.[11] Each of these movements had confronted American Christians in nearly all churches and denominations in all regions of the country for over a century. The following critical description of the Holiness movement made in an address by a bishop before the 1894 General Conference of the Methodist Episcopal Church illustrates how new movements upset old churches:

> There has sprung up among us a party with holiness as a watchword; they have holiness associations, holiness meetings, holiness preachers, holiness evangelists, and holiness property. . . . Such terms as "saints," "sanctified," are restricted to the few who have reached the height of perfect purity and improperly denied to the body of believers. . . . We deplore their teaching and methods in so far as they claim a monopoly of the experience, practice, and advocacy of holiness, and separate themselves from the body of ministers and disciples.[12]

The new movements, and new churches that grew out of the movements, often became exclusive communities of highly distinctive forms of Christian identity. Each has been certain of owning the vital key to true Christianity. With a witness to *the truth* in a society of many religions competing for believers, these aggressive new Christian movements grew rapidly. They fed on converts from older congregations, and as "comeouters" they separated themselves from the large traditional churches. In this way they contributed many new entries to the list that makes up American religious pluralism.

Throughout the nineteenth century, European

observers of the American scene commented on the unprecedented variety of religious life in this new nation. They mixed their criticism of the peculiarities of American church life and thought with respect for the enthusiasm and growth of the various Christian groups. Some feared for cherished traditions, and for social order, in a land where religion freely went its haphazard way. Frances Trollope, the loyal Anglican critic of the United States which she visited during the late 1820's, clearly preferred the way of an established church as "the bulwark which protects us [but not Americans] from the gloomy horrors of fanatic superstition on one side, and the still more dreadful inroads of infidelity on the other side."[13]

It is difficult to find nineteenth-century American Christians who really celebrated the religious diversity in their midst. Even those most excited about religious freedom deplored the lack of unifying forces among the many churches. Where was *the church* in the midst of the many churches? Responses varied. One popular answer envisaged an evangelical Protestant Christendom made up of the cooperative association of the major denominations (discussed in Chapter 4, below). But this cooperative unity excluded as many Christians as it included. It tended to focus on the common denominator of Christian beliefs around which all might unite. The problem was that within each tradition there were those who located the essence of Christianity at particular points not shared by others. Consequently different conceptions of the basis for Christian unity only served to exaggerate the divisions.

Roman Catholics insisted on religious allegiance to the Roman papacy as the essential unity. High Church Episcopalians could find unity only within their concept of the historic episcopacy. Landmark Baptists recognized true Christianity only in the historic succession of congregations of baptized adult believers. Disciples of Christ wanted to unite all Christians within their concept of primitive New Testament associations of believers. Lutherans looked to their historic "conservative" Reformation confessions, while Presbyterians and other Reformed churches held fast to certain doctrines of Biblical authority and historic creeds. Methodists made a combination of a particular "strange heart-warmed experience" and moral teachings the true grounds for Christian unity. In each case Christianity became reduced to some particular emphasis as most important. The problem was that others did not agree.

Could a nation hold together with no sense of religious commonality? Could churches maintain their fundamental integrity, or even survive in recognizable form, amid such unbridled license? These questions, asked by European-oriented church persons in the Old World and the New, could be answered only with the passage of time. There was no real precedent to the American situation.

Meanwhile it was apparent that America proved to be fertile soil for the flowering of all kinds of particular forms of imported Christianity. By the middle of the nineteenth century the German Reformed immigrant, Philip Schaff, who was on the faculty of the small seminary in Mercersburg,

Pennsylvania, could describe religion in America to his colleagues in Germany in these enduring words:

> Favored by the general freedom of faith, all Christian denominations and sects, except for the Oriental, have settled in the United States, on equal footing in the eye of the law; here attracting each other, there repelling; rivalling in both the good and the bad sense; and mutually contending through innumerable religious publications. They thus present a motley sampler of all church history, and the results it has thus far attained.[14]

Eventually the "Oriental" religious groups would also join the crowd.

The American ideals of democracy, of "grassroots individualism," of people "doing their own thing," have contributed to the multiplicity of religious life. A certain tendency toward extremism (ultraism, to use the historical term), meaning people's enthusiastic advocacy of convictions and causes, has accompanied religious freedom. Individualism and aggressiveness can be attributed in part to the kind of people hearty and determined enough to migrate across an ocean to begin a new life on another continent. After they arrived, their creativity and enthusiasm were further challenged. They had to reaffirm their beliefs in a new setting amid many religious alternatives and much religious competition.

Nineteenth-century quests for Christian identity found countless outlets and limitless expressions in America. There were ample possibilities for a measure of separateness and religious ex-

perimentation, always the freedom and space to
go somewhere and organize religiously. In addition to traditional churches dividing, America's
history is filled with the constant springing up of
new religious groups. Some were small, localized,
and short-lived. Others grew rapidly, became
widespread and permanent. Diversity has fostered
diversity; individualism has fostered individualism; and freedom not to conform has fostered nonconformity.

2

Christians Estranged: Patterns of Withdrawal and Subculture

Deeply ingrained in the American religious experience is the "retreat." Persons leave the normal circumstances of their complicated lives and go into temporary seclusion in order to concentrate on their nature and purpose as a group and to gain spiritual renewal.

Revivalism has functioned as a kind of mass retreat where emotional preaching for conversions and "testimonies" of spiritual "new birth" evoked traumatic religious experiences in large-group contexts. Evangelical identity thereby was reaffirmed. A more esoteric mode of retreat has been the ashram, a quiet, small-group revival in which persons spend long periods of time working through their spiritual needs and experiences together. But the most common form of retreat has been one in which members of a church community take several days in a country-like setting to renew their spirit, plan their programs, and generally solidify their common sense of Christian identity. Then they return to their normal surroundings and life-styles as the "church in the world" both gathered and dispersed.

Some Christians, however, have discovered and expressed their identity in permanent retreat—a religious withdrawal from the world. This too is part of the American religious experience.

CHRISTIAN WITHDRAWAL

For those so inclined, America has provided the space and the opportunity to seek religious identity in isolation from the social, political, and economic world about them. For some, isolation meant simply to "live and let live." For others it meant keeping religion in its proper place. For still others it meant striving for perfection. However motivated, Americans have found their own distinctive versions of the aged practice of religious withdrawal.

The expression of Christian identity through personal and communal withdrawal from society never has been absent from church history. During the centuries of European Christendom the church provided monastic orders for those inclined to "leave the world." Their ascetic (self-denying) life not only was legitimated by the church; it was also highly respected as meriting special religious blessings. But this was true only so long as it remained within the control of ecclesiastical authority. Groups asserting their independence from the official church were proclaimed heretical and treated as renegade separatists or schismatics. This usually led to persecution and suppression.

With the breakup of ecclesiastical unity in the

sixteenth century, various forms of radical Christian separatism found new life. Reformation radicalism flourished in all areas of Christian life and thought. Most of these groups tended to pattern themselves after the ideals they perceived in primitive Christianity of the first and second centuries. They traced the "fall" of the church to Emperor Constantine, when "Christianity ascended the throne of the Caesars" in the fourth century and became identified with all of society as the state religion.

According to this interpretation of history, most true Christians existed in underground movements during the centuries of Christendom. Usually they were camouflaged in church history, becoming publicly visible as victims of persecution when in conflict with civil and ecclesiastical authorities. But they persevered as the company of true believers who had shunned the corrupt worldly life in which the official church was mired. This was *sectarian* Christianity, sharply distinguished from *churchly* religion.[1]

Radical Puritans brought some of these separatist tendencies to colonial America. In England they were nonconformists who dissented from ecclesiastical and civil authority. But Puritans were not fundamentally isolationist in their outlook. Even as they described their New England "Bible Commonwealths" as "cities on a hill" in contrast to Old World civilization and its ecclesiastical structures, their long-range goal was to renovate the world in their own Christian image.

For example, the Puritans tried to maintain an exclusive church membership made up of regenerate believers. In this way they acted like a separatist sect; the seeds of religious withdrawal were planted among them. Yet they also insisted that their church, and only their church, should take responsibility for all of society. Hence they tried to maintain the comprehensive, all-inclusive church of Christendom. They meant to be "visible saints" practicing a "this-worldly asceticism," and as such they projected a Christian identity which held the church-sect extremes in precariously balanced tension. Furthermore, they bequeathed this tension to subsequent American Christianity. Whereas the primary influence of New England Puritanism has come through the public force of the nation's major Protestant denominations, it also has made an impact through various forms of separatism.

The Quakers are a good example of how Puritanism could lead to experimentation in community withdrawal. During the American Revolution the Quaker movement went into a period of quietistic separatism which lasted for half a century. Quakers had originated in the seventeenth century as a radical and aggressive Puritan sect. Their bold nonconformity in areas of theology, worship, ethics, and church organization provoked the established churches in old and New England into harsh retaliatory measures. By the eighteenth century, Quakers had succeeded in coexisting in relative peace with less radical Puritans and other religious groups. In Pennsylvania, Quakers became deeply entrenched in the social, political, and economic power structures.

During the Revolution, however, Quakers lost

much of their hard-earned public favor and influence. Pacifist by tradition and conviction, they had
been unenthusiastic about the war. Many remained loyalists, some fleeing the nation, others
staying on as quiet dissenters. Not all Quakers opposed the war, of course; some gave full support.
But the movement as a whole responded by with-
drawing, except in business matters, into isolation
from the world about them. They even tried to
practice endogamous marriage in an effort to preserve the purity of their tradition and the clarity
of their identity.

Introspection always has been at the heart of the
Quaker experience. The tradition has practiced a
style of silent corporate worship—the quiet seeking for the inner light which dwells within each
person. But outside of worship they were not an
exceptionally introverted people. Indeed, their inner light experience drove them outward with an
activist concern for justice and reform in the
world. "Quakerism was born with a passion for a
better social world."[2] Moreover, Quaker roots
were too Puritan to allow them much satisfaction
in a situation of withdrawal from society. Having
originally struggled against being cast out of society, they could not retain their essential identity in
isolation from society once accepted into it.

By the second quarter of the nineteenth century, Quakers were taking roles in the public
affairs of American life. Always they had wit-
nessed, often alone, against violence and slavery in
colonial society. Now they became involved in
movements of antislavery, peace, women's rights,
prison reform, and other social issues. Some Quak-

ers even participated in public revivalism, over which they, like everyone else, became divided.

Quaker identity, after all, was not essentially isolationist or communitarian. As the Society of Friends they became a permanent and publicly respected American Christian denomination. For the past half century the American Friends Service Committee has been a major instrument of social creativity for these mystics of public social conscience.

A more extreme and enduring example of isolated communal Christianity that developed during the period of the American Revolution are the Shakers. Having immigrated to America in 1774 after experiencing persecution in England, this handful of sectarian Christians followed the leadership of Mother Ann Lee into a kind of Protestant monastic experiment. Mother Ann became convinced that Christ had "come again" in feminine form within herself, and that those who would experience Christ's second coming in their lives must withdraw from the world into a disciplined communal life of celibacy, worship, and work—a "heaven on earth life."[3]

Communities of religious fervor were formed in western New York State and in several New England states. Since Shakers were celibate, their communities grew only by adult conversion and by the adoption of orphan children. Their greatest size of about six thousand members was reached in the middle of the nineteenth century. Their disciplined worship featured a mild shaking dance movement to hymn singing (shaking sin from their lives), and open confession of sin. All property was owned in common, and communities were self-supporting. Basically farmers, Shakers became famous for their useful inventions, their seed business, their architecture, and their design and production of furniture.

After the Civil War, America's urban-industrial revolution made Shaker communities less attractive and profitable, and slowly they dwindled in size and disbanded. Celebrating their bicentennial in 1974, the handful of remaining Shakers have decided to "close the adventure" and admit no new members.[4] Only in isolation could Shaker identity remain intact.

Many other communal Christian experiments of briefer duration took form during the early years of the American Republic. As Americans began their westward movement out of New England and other Atlantic states, traveling either across the old Southwest or through the Ohio River valley via the Erie Canal, they left scattered about a variety of communal religious experiments. Some sought moral perfection, others utopias; still others awaited Christ's quick return. The Society of the Public Universal Friend, the Oneida Community, the Millerites, the Spiritualites, the Rappites, New Harmony, the Separatists of Zoar, the Amana Society, and the Transcendentalist communities of Fruitlands, Brook Farm, and Hopedale are illustrations of what was happening.

The pattern thus was set for the continual bursting forth of new Christian groups in America, often conceived as experiments, gathering into communal refuges from society-at-large, seeking a particular identity within the nation.

Roman Catholics mixed tradition with novelty in their ventures into communal isolation during the antebellum period. Trusteeism (laypersons acting in church affairs on their own initiative)[5] became the Catholic version of American tendencies toward local congregational autonomy which challenged traditional hierarchical controls. As in most larger Protestant denominations, traditional patterns of regional and national Catholic Church control eventually qualified such localism, and Christians became integrated into the developing national public life.

Meanwhile, regularized forms of Catholic monastic communities found their place within the nation. The Trappists, for example, came to the United States as early as 1802, fleeing persecution under the anticlerical laws following the French Revolution. Their first permanent monastery, after decades of abortive attempts, was established in 1848 near Bardstown, Kentucky. Several Trappist monasteries exist in America today, maintaining vows of poverty, celibacy, silence, and withdrawal from the world.

More innovative as an American mode of Christian communal identity was the German Catholic Brotherhood, made up of immigrant families in Philadelphia and Baltimore seeking rural seclusion from the tensions and confusion of urban life. They found a spot in the forests of northwestern Pennsylvania, secured assistance first from the Redemptorists, later from the German Benedictines who were more experienced farmers, and named their pioneer mission-settlement St. Mary's. They provided schools for children and in every way tried to maintain their identity in self-supportive isolation from public life. They became one of the most successful of such immigrant frontier communities in America during the 1840's and 1850's. Their Christian objectives within the nation were vividly described in a letter by one of their Redemptorist consultants, reading in part as follows:

> I believe that I can see in the new establishment the future refuge where this infant Christianity sheltered from the corruption of the world and perversion of heresy, will increase in knowledge without losing virtue and will furnish generous vocations among which God will be pleased to choose Apostles for America. It seems to me that thousands of Catholics will yet rally around the cross as around the religious symbol of true liberty. I already foresee a nascent congregation, a humble daughter of the universal Church, flowering in the desert beneath the divine benediction. . . . There is the place, I think, that henceforth we will point out to the German Catholics who arrive on these distant shores and who remain in the cities of this country only long enough to obtain the necessary money to acquire a piece of land; it is there that they will be able to earn their living and at the same time preserve their faith and save their souls.[6]

Among Protestants, the most enduring tradition of isolated community life in America has been expressed by the Mennonites and the Amish. These people have understood their isolation, not as an experiment or a temporary state, but as their inherited and natural form of family and church-centered life. They trace their heritage to the radical sectarian "left wing" of the sixteenth-century Protestant Reformation. Originally known as Ana-baptists (rebaptizers), they distinguished them-selves from Calvinist and Lutheran state-church traditions by refusing to be involved in public life. Rejecting the whole concept and history of Chris-tendom, they identified with primitive Christian-ity prior to the Emperor Constantine's establish-ment of the church as the imperial religion. They therefore rejected infant baptism, the act solidify-ing citizenship in the civil order with the official church membership, and instead baptized adult believers into congregations separate from state churches.

Persecuted by Protestants and Catholics alike, these people wandered throughout Europe, into Russia, some migrating to the New World, where especially in Canada and the United States they found refuge and freedom to live their isolated communal life in relative peace. Their communi-ties have been planted throughout rural America, in several varieties and degrees of isolation, but each with a distinct sense of Christian identity al-most void of reference to American nationality ex-cept as a place to live freely and separately among their own.

With common historical roots, the Mennonites and the Amish have continued to share many con-victions in America. Both groups center their life in their understanding of the Bible. Both attempt to live in simplicity, in obedience (discipleship to Christ), and in mutual love. Both groups believe that the Christian life is separated from "worldly" activities and customs and that the church must have nothing to do with civil government. Both communities strive to be self-contained and self-supporting. They provide their own social activities, education, and system of mutual aid to alleviate suffering from disasters for their members.

Mennonites understand themselves to be communities of "the saved," a "peculiar people" called out from the sinful world to live in isolated communities governed according to the New Testament concept of love. Though exceptions can be found, generally Mennonites have stayed outside of politics, civil offices, and the military. They have refused to take civil oaths or to initiate lawsuits. They remain aloof from public elections, though some do vote. Yet they strongly believe in obeying the laws of society, except when a law specifically conflicts with their religious belief and confrontation is unavoidable. As strict pacifists, for example, they have refused to participate in warfare, and because of this they have suffered much abuse during the past two centuries. Under the Conscription Act of 1940 they were able to accept peaceful alternative service unrelated to military activity (40 percent of all conscientious objectors during World War II were Mennonites). Since then, Mennonites frequently have given testimony against war and conscription in the nation's capital. In this manner they have come to make visible public witness to their deepest religious convictions about corporate human life. But these expressions of a social conscience have qualified the degree of their communal isolation.

The Mennonites and the Amish have not followed identical paths in America. Today they differ in the degree to which they have accommodated to modern culture. Mennonites feel that they practice the ethics of Jesus in a sinful world more closely than do the large Christian denominations. Yet outwardly Mennonites are "an anomaly in society—at once not yet adjusted to it and in advance of it." Compared to the Amish they have gone "half worldly," however, by worshiping in church buildings, maintaining their own colleges, conducting missionary activities, publishing literature, and administering worldwide relief services.

The Amish reject all these modern American "innovations" and hold fast to their seventeenth-century customs, dress, and general life-style. Some even refused to use such modern inventions as automobiles, tractors, telephones, and electric lights. They have refused to pay Social Security taxes on the grounds that they, not the government, are responsible for the care of their own aged members. (The Amish pay income and property taxes.) They make no attempt to convert outsiders to their communal ways of life and thought.

> According to them the greatest wisdom is to despise the world and to love God. To seek wealth and to rely upon it is worldly. . . . To pursue honors or high dignity and to "raise oneself" through fashionable dress, education, office-holding, or any other way is worldly. To provide adequate sustenance for the family is necessary, but luxuries and superfluities and lustful appetites the Amishman regards as harmful to the soul.[7]

With remarkable success the Mennonites, and especially the Amish, have isolated themselves from much of the material and intellectual culture of modernity surrounding their communities (though leakage of younger members into that outer world has not been uncommon in recent years). Everything considered, they have been an extreme example of communal Christian isolation from public life in American history.

Religious withdrawal from the larger life of society has been expressed more generally in American Christianity than immediately is apparent. It has existed not only in the form of striking communitarian experiments or permanent physical isolation from public life but also in religious isolation from the world of religions. Some have attempted to preserve their sense of being the true expression of Christianity within the American pluralistic environment by isolating themselves from all other churches. But most churches have recognized the possibility, at least, of true believers residing in other communions. Few have taken the extreme position of the Jehovah's Witnesses, for example. This separatistic and exclusivist sect of "spiritual elite" has repudiated *all* other Christian churches and movements as thoroughly false. The repudiation has been symbolized in "withdrawal letters" which converts send to their former congregations in order to explain their reasons for "quitting Babylon."[8]

The tendency to isolate religion from "worldly life," however, has been a powerful force within even the large traditional American churches. Many Christians believe that religion has a sphere of its own, distinct from the world of politics, economics, and social issues. They therefore isolate

their religion from their involvement in these
large public arenas where much of American life
takes place. But unlike the Mennonites, for example, these "mainstream" Christians do not separate their religious-centered lives from modern society. Rather, they separate religion from much of
the center of their lives.

Often the question has been asked in America,
Should the church meddle in civil affairs? The
word "meddle" betrays the answer. Typical was
the emphatic answer "No" given in 1966 by J.
Howard Pew, the prominent Sun Oil Company
executive and national officer in The United Presbyterian Church in the U.S.A. Pew believed that
individual Christians should speak out and act in
secular society according to their Christian con-
sciences where "moral and spiritual principles are
clearly involved." But churches as such should remain aloof from public life, lest they become divided.

> Action to correct existing ills in secular society
> should be taken through secular organizations: po-
> litical parties, chambers of commerce, labor un-
> ions, parent-teacher associations, service clubs and
> many others which can supply skilled leadership
> and techniques to do the jobs.[9]

Pew's use of the word "secular" is important, for
in one sense he was responding positively to the
secularization of America. In its technical historical definition secularization is the process whereby
Christian institutions and symbols cease to participate in sectors of society and culture.[10] By this
definition secularity implies that certain dimen-

sions of human life fall outside the proper activities of churches.

Yet the very notion that churches have their proper place is also part of the heritage of Western Christendom. Christendom and secularization are intertwined, as one historical epoch merging into another. As we shall see in Chapter 4, many Christians have presupposed that Christendom lived on in America. They have assumed that America fundamentally is a Christian civilization wherein the churches have their ordered and proper place.

It is when the Christendom outlook combines with the acceptance of secularization that a common kind of religious isolation occurs. Churches do not become involved in social problems because they assume that the religious and the secular are two distinct spheres of life which ought to be kept separate. Yet these same churches may also assume that American institutions and social structures are essentially Christian. All that is needed is the moral strengthening of individual citizens, which is where the church comes in. Persons taking this position have limited the role of the churches to the "spiritual" business of "soul-saving" and personal morality. When enough souls are saved and begin living righteous lives, so the argument goes, then the Christian nature of society automatically will be enhanced.

In Chapter 5, we shall see how wrong some of these assumptions have turned out to be. American society is not essentially Christian, the saving of individual souls does not automatically reform society, and the churches have no proper and ordered place in a free and secular society. Perhaps most important to persons who struggle with the problem of Christian identity is this fact: as Christendom disintegrates, religion kept within certain spheres of life leaves a religious void in other spheres. Ironically, to isolate religion even for the purpose of maintaining its strength and integrity is to bolster the process of secularization.

Religious isolation, however, has not always happened by the believers' preference. Not all Christians have experienced the opportunity to express their identity in American life to the extent that they have desired. They have been forced to withdraw into relatively isolated minority subcultures within which their churches have provided the focus of identity and, at times, of survival.

CHRISTIAN MINORITY SUBCULTURES

Prejudice, discrimination, and bigotry have played their roles in American history. Racial, ethnic, and religious minorities have been the victims. For them to be Christian and American without abandoning their cultural identities has been a painful uphill battle. They have suffered the stigma of nonconformity, partly by coercion and partly on their own initiative.

Where state churches ruled in colonial America, nonconformists frequently were banished to the wilderness. No such legal measures could be taken against unpopular Christian groups after the Federal Constitution took effect (although there have been instances of mass deportations of Americans innocent of any crimes). But Americans found other ways to make life difficult for the "undesirables" and to minimize their public influence.

Some Christians were pushed outside the mainstream of society. They organized their church-centered lives in the form of highly distinctive moral, spiritual, and ideological alternatives to the prevailing American culture. It is important to note that those churches which society tried hard to camouflage persevered on their own terms. They became strong enough to survive not simply in private isolation but also through their indomitable protrusions into the public social order on the strength of their own distinctive identities. Indeed, their Christianity penetrated so deeply and comprehensively into their individual and corporate lives that they can best be understood as Christian minority subcultures.[11]

It is one of the ironies of American church history that two of the major indigenous Christian traditions were ostracized to such an extent that they developed cultural-religious identities unique to themselves. These were the Mormons and the black churches. They have been almost totally separated from other Christian traditions. The irony is magnified by the fact that a historic Mormon Church doctrine excluding black persons from the church's priesthood has presented a particular barrier between Mormons and black Christians. (There are some black members of the Mormon Church.) These two major American religious subcultures, therefore, have been even more separated from each other than each has been estranged from the rest of American Christianity. The two have had little in common apart from their similar modes of identity as distinctive minority Christian cultures alongside of, and quite separate from, the dominant social life of the nation.

The Mormons

The Mormon Church—properly, the Church of Jesus Christ of Latter-day Saints—was born during the revivals in western New York in the 1820's and 1830's. Joseph Smith was the founder and first prophet of the church which was legally organized on April 6, 1830. That same year Joseph Smith first published his translation of the Book of Mormon.

By Smith's testimony, he had discovered the text of the Book of Mormon engraved on gold plates. According to the text, these plates had been left by an ancient civilization of the period 600 B.C. to A.D. 421. These people of Asiatic origin and of the House of Israel left Jerusalem, crossed the sea, and developed a civilization in what now is North America. The gold plates contained records of these ancient people, whom the text identifies as having been among the ancestors of the American Indians. The text also witnesses that Jesus Christ appeared among this North American people after his ascension.

Furthermore, the Book of Mormon foretells Columbus' discovery of America, the fate of Indians with the coming of Europeans to the American "land of promise," the Puritans who enjoyed "the power of the Lord," and the American Revolution in which "the Gentiles that had gone out of [Old World] captivity were delivered by the power of God out of the hands of all other nations."

And this land shall be a land of liberty unto the
Gentiles, and there shall be no kings upon the land,
who shall raise up unto the Gentiles. And I will
fortify this land against all other nations.[12]

Therefore Mormons experienced a unique relationship to the New World unshared by other
Christians. Their sacred literature in the Book of
Mormon complemented the Old and New Testa-
ments of the Bible. They identified with a sacred
history that tied ancient Israel and Jesus Christ to
the New World. By accepting this new American
Christian revelation, the basis of their "restored"
church, Mormons set themselves apart from all
other Christians. Called out from among the
American "Gentiles" (non-Mormons), Mormons
identified themselves as "Saints." America, land of
liberty for all, held special promise for the "Saints"
of this "latter day." But Mormons also were isolated from the mainstream of nineteenth-century
American life by the persecution and banishment
they experienced wherever they tried to settle.

Mormons suffered hostility especially from Protestants, whose ancestral roots they shared. Joseph
Smith's family history had deep New England
Protestant roots. Mormonism contained much of
the spirit of the Puritan-evangelical tradition—the
public moral discipline, the centrality of sacred
scripture, the sacramental reverence for corporate singing and the spoken word, the sense of
being a chosen people of providence, the aggressive missionary zeal. Moreover, the Book of Mormon spoke authoritatively to nearly every theological and ecclesiastical issue in which nineteenth-
century American Protestants were embroiled. It

partly was this absoluteness in religious matters
which attracted converts away from those Protestant churches whose competition and controversy
ran rampant in the free religious atmosphere of
nineteenth-century America. The persuasive Mormon answers elicited the hostility of Protestant
church leaders.

Even more threatening to Protestants were
Mormon novelties: a new revealed scripture, continuing revelation through human leaders of near-
absolute authority, the practice of polygamy, and
numerous doctrinal formulations covering everything from the nature of God to baptism to marriage and family life. As a communal movement
with "peculiar" beliefs and practices which they
identified as *the* true Christianity, Mormons separated themselves from other Christians. The other
Christians, holding fast to more orthodox traditions, judged Mormonism to be so full of heresy as
to be in fact a new religion. Protestants often lik-
ened Mormons to Moslems vis-à-vis medieval
Christianity—"Mormonism the Islam of America."[13]

The Mormons preferred to think of themselves
as the reformers and culminators of Christianity,
much as early Christians had identified themselves
with regard to Judaism. The Church of Jesus Christ
of Latter-day Saints was to express the fullness of
Christianity for the new age. All other churches
were but partial expressions of Christianity at best.
Mormons believed in universal salvation, but "ex-
altation" in the eternal Kingdom of God would be
reserved for those who obeyed the laws and com-
mandments of that Kingdom as most fully ex-

pressed in Mormonism. On this basis the Mormons proselytized aggressively wherever they settled. Their converts joined a community consciously separated from other Christians and withdrawn from society-at-large.

Mormons were driven out of New York, Ohio, Missouri, Illinois, and eventually California. In 1844, Joseph Smith was murdered by a mob in Carthage, Illinois. Under the new leadership of Brigham Young, the Mormons began their dramatic trek westward. They found a permanent place to settle in the valley of the great Salt Lake in the Utah Territory—the new promised land "that nobody wanted." Here at "the crossroads of the West" they flourished as a kind of territorial Christian empire during the later nineteenth century. In their "new Zion" they developed a unique religious culture on the outskirts of the nation. Though estranged from the national culture, they identified deeply with America.

As the nation expanded westward, "Gentiles" increasingly mixed with Mormon "Saints" in Utah. "Gentiles" expressed fears that the ultimate goal of the Mormons was to bring their church into political control not only of Utah but of the entire country. The Federal Government responded to anti-Mormon fears by means of antipolygamy legislation, prosecution of offenders, legal dissolution of the church's incorporation and property, and the revoking of Mormons' political rights. Meanwhile, statehood was withheld from Utah until 1896.

When church president Wilford Woodruff issued his dramatic 1898 "Manifesto" repudiating the practice of polygamy, the Americanization of Mormonism had begun (an ironic process for an indigenous American religious tradition). Eventually the church regained its freedom, its property, and its strength, but at the cost of some accommodation to the nation's dominant cultural patterns. Partly in reaction to anti-Mormon propaganda early in the twentieth century, Mormons tightened the bonds of their communal identity while assuming a stance of extreme American patriotism. (Their American loyalty during World War I countered the anti-Mormon movement.) "Defeated in conflict with the general American community and the federal government," writes one perceptive scholar, the Mormon Church "had to reconcile itself to that general community, but it continued to assert its own particular values in that general context."[14]

Mormonism has spread throughout the nation and in many parts of the world. It is highly organized in geographical "stakes" and "wards." The church penetrates nearly all areas of its members' lives. It has developed an organized social welfare program in which Mormons can take care of their own. It offers an elaborate religious education program in which Mormons might solidify their faith and their sense of identity. It permeates family life and keeps track of "renegade" members wherever they wander or settle. It promotes a moral code and ideological framework to govern its adherents' lives in the present world and the next. In this way Mormons have become integrated into American life while retaining a clear sense of particular Christian identity distinct from other Christians.

We have noted that Mormons historically made a racial distinction with regard to the priesthood. Black persons are excluded from that office. Race relations was one of the many conflicts raging within and among the early-nineteenth-century churches which Mormons tried to solve by doctrinal decree. Mormons were no more or less racist in their attitudes toward black people than were other white American Christians. Most other white churches have generally excluded black persons from clerical roles in practice, if not in theory, until recent years. But as a new church based on new revelation, the Mormons' exclusion of black persons from the priesthood spoke with a sacred finality to "the race question." This exclusion became part of the church's fundamental doctrine which would haunt the Mormon community in later years when American racial attitudes changed.

Today white Mormon Church leaders must struggle with the tension between their doctrine and their changing attitudes toward black Americans. This struggle is illustrated in the following statement issued by church president Harold B. Lee on December 5, 1969:

> From the beginning of this dispensation, Joseph Smith and all succeeding presidents of the church have taught that Negroes, while spirit children of a common Father, and the progeny of our earthly parents, Adam and Eve, were not yet to receive

the priesthood for reasons which we believe are known to God, but which He has not made fully known to man.

According to President Lee, "sometime in God's eternal plan the Negro will be given the right to hold the priesthood."[15]

The Black Churches

To black American Christians, the Mormon version of "God's eternal plan" for black equality with white has been but a variation of a theme sung by white churches in general. Black people systematically have been restricted from full participation in the mainstream of social, economic, and political life in America—including church life. Consequently those black persons who have identified themselves as Christians as well as Americans have done so as a subculture within which the other major indigenous form of American Christianity has emerged and flourished—the black churches.

Nineteenth-century black American Christians, like the Mormons, identified with the New World uniquely. Both communities visualized their special destinies within the nation, distinguishing themselves from other Americans. The destiny of each would require a great historic turnabout in which the oppressed would be liberated and exalted. Both looked to the past, to ancient Israel, for inspiration and vision of the future. Otherwise the present appeared alien to their fondest aspirations.

At this point the similarity between the Mormon

and the black American subculture broke down. They lived in different worlds. Mormons freely chose their religious and social orientation, though not their persecution. They were converts to a Christian identity in America which largely contributed to their place in society. But black Christians began as slaves. Even after emancipation they suffered oppression because of the skin color with which they were born. Christian identity made little difference in how black persons were treated, though Christian faith made a great deal of difference in how a black person related to the experience of oppression.

Black slaves confronted a white Christianity which persistently told them to accept their bondage passively and humbly. From the white church came the apostle Paul's admonition: "Servants, be obedient to them that are your masters" (Eph. 6:5). After the Civil War, when slavery no longer could be upheld by Scriptural reference, the same passage frequently was quoted to keep black people "in their place." For a black person to identify with this kind of Christianity, therefore, meant to accept sacred endorsement of a second-class American citizenship. Small wonder that many slaves, and freedmen, rejected Christian faith outright.

But many others became Christians. Through contact with white plantation owners, and as the subjects of Protestant church missions, black people were converted to Christianity throughout their long period of slavery in America. Their Christianity differed markedly from that preached to them from white churches. It is essential to note

two primary factors that uniquely conditioned the
black Christians' sense of Christian identity in
America: (1) they were an enslaved and oppressed
people, and (2) they came with an African rather
than a European cultural heritage.

1. Unlike most immigrants, black people came
unwillingly to the New World as slaves in chains.
Unlike European immigrants, Africans did not
come to America for social, political, economic, or
religious freedom. To the contrary, Africans lost
their freedom in America. Consequently they
could not identify with Christianity as the arena in
which freedom had been won. Christianity was
the arena in which they became slaves. Africans
knew less freedom in America than Europeans
had known in Christendom under the worst of
conditions.

Black American slaves accepted and understood
the Christian gospel as a promise of liberation to
the oppressed. No other American Christians
could share the black perspective, for no others
shared the black enslavement as a people. The
slaves identified personally with the ancient Isra-
elites who were led by Moses out of bondage in
Egypt, across the river Jordan, into a new promised land. The slaves would become a new Israel,
God's oppressed people, whose deliverance would
come *from* and *within* America. Across their own
"deep river," a deliverance from the white masters and their slave system would come. Black
slaves identified with Jesus in their suffering, and
they anticipated eternal salvation after death with
Jesus. This would be their ultimate liberation and
their final home. But their otherworldly hopes

never obliterated their hopes for physical liberation in this world.

Hence black slaves were the victims, not the benefactors, of American society. They could not fully, if at all, identify with American nationality, for they did not share in basic American civil rights. "What to the American slave is your Fourth of July?" asked freedman Frederick Douglass in a speech he delivered in Rochester, New York, on July 4, 1852.

> What to the American slave is your Fourth of July? I answer, a day that reveals to him more than all other days of the year, the gross injustice and cruelty to which he is the constant victim. To him your celebration is a sham; your boasted liberty an unholy license; your national greatness, swelling vanity; your sounds of rejoicing are empty and heartless; your denunciation of tyrants, brass-fronted impudence; your shouts of liberty and equality, hollow mockery; your prayers and hymns, your sermons and thanksgivings, with all your religious parade and solemnity, are to him mere bombast, fraud, deception, impiety, and hypocrisy—a thin veil to cover up crimes which would disgrace a nation of savages.[16]

Frederick Douglass spoke eloquently for enslaved black Americans who experienced "the immeasurable distance" between themselves and white citizens. To this oppressed people the Civil War could only mean divine intervention in American history. Through the Emancipation Proclamation, God's oppressed people were delivered from bondage. So preached black Californian Ezra Johnson in an 1867 Emancipation Day ora-

tion: "God has been our leader, and we have
passed through the Red Sea, and now rejoice that
Canaan is in view."[17]

But Canaan was long in coming. With the break-
down of the Reconstruction, black people in the
South became victims of a rigidly segregated and
discriminatory culture of white supremacy. As rac-
ism permeated white churches, black Christians
developed their own churches and denominations
—most of them Baptist or Methodist.

Nor did the North prove to be the promised
land. Black people who migrated into Northern
cities, seeking freedom and employment, suffered
from racist discrimination no less severe than they
had known in the South. Indeed the urban-industrial revolution subjected black people to new
forms of injustice. Recent immigrants, struggling
for jobs in industry, viewed black people as com-
petitors. During labor strikes, management often
hired black newcomers as scabs, which increased
white laborers' hostility toward black people.
Strike settlements meant loss of jobs for black
workers. Many labor unions operated on white
racist policies which excluded blacks from membership. Hence black people became victims of
injustice by labor and management alike, leaving
them with virtually no economic power base.
They found no more relief from oppression in
Northern industrial society than on Southern plan-
tations. Urban slum ghettos became the environ-
mental context of the black religious subculture.

Victims of discrimination socially, politically,
economically, and religiously, black Americans developed their sense of identity from within a sub-

culture. The black churches became the heart of this subculture. The churches became the one institution in black community experience not controlled somehow by white society. Far from separatist or ascetic in nature, these churches (with notable exceptions) have participated in the fullness of "this-worldly" life by engaging in every aspect of the black community's struggle for social, economic, and political survival.

Christianity therefore has been a central ingredient in the black community's sense of identity in America. The identity of the blacks as Christians and as Americans has been determined by their blackness, making them distinct among Christians and among Americans—"a religion within a religion in a nation within a nation." Black American Christians have known the sting of W. E. B. Du Bois' question (1903): "Why did God make me an outcast and a stranger in mine own house?" As outcasts they expressed nobly their identity as a Christian "underculture" with the "double-consciousness of . . . being Black in White America."[18]

2. Black Christian identity in America cannot be understood, finally, apart from the African heritage of black people. As a unique blend of African religions with European-rooted evangelical Protestantism, American black Christianity is indigenous to the New World. The mixture of African religion with Protestantism was not imported to America; it originated in America under slave conditions. Whereas European-rooted Christianity permeated the dominant cultural traditions and social institutions in America, African-rooted religion in America had to exist more as an under-

ground movement in a minority subculture almost invisible to white society.

The black churches therefore emerged from within the black community, which was separated from and largely ignored by white American Christians. This was a new form of American Christianity whose foundation was African religion with European religion added.

> It is far more accurate to speak of Blackamerican Christianity as a point on a continuum beginning in Africa, than to speak of it as the direct descendent of a tradition beginning in Athens or Rome or, for that matter, England. The European was grafted onto the African, and not vice versa.

Furthermore, "the African slave was the author of the adaptations."[19]

During the period of slavery, African religion provided a foundation for the expression of black Christianity. Christian slaves frequently worshiped in secret meetings, where they could express their deepest religious instincts and sense of cultural heritage. After emancipation, the black churches became the locus of Afro-American religion with its own theological orientation, worship forms, pastoral style, and organizational structures. This African heritage, combined with the segregation of black people from white society, therefore maintained the rich religious subculture within which black American Christians have asserted their sense of identity.

As we shall see in the next chapter, it finally has been through asserting their civil rights and their racial pride that black Christians have most clearly realized their identity as Americans.

3

Christian Dissent:
Racial, Sexual,
and Foreign Assertiveness

Dissent has been a fundamental expression of American religious freedom. Most Americans who identify even remotely with a particular Christian tradition are aware of some dissenting note in their ancestral past, if not in their own lives.

In contrast to medieval Christendom, American religious dissent has not automatically been illegal, dangerous, or even unpopular. Indeed, one of the implications of the American religious revolution was "to place both orthodoxy and dissent upon the same shifting platforms of public favor and public support."[1] Nevertheless, religious dissent has had its peculiarly American sting, vigor, and consistency. Certain Christians, among others, have identified themselves as dissenters with great insistence.

People dissent from religious doctrines, practices, and structures that they find oppressive, false, or otherwise unacceptable. They may simply withhold their assent to authority in quiet disobedience; they may separate from the association and go their own ways; or they may become advocates and fomenters of change. The history of American Christianity is full of these various forms of dissent. The story can be told with regard to internal conflicts, external schisms, and movements for reform.

Christians also have dissented from actions and conditions of the public civil order. As individuals and as religious interest groups they have opposed oppression and civil injustices of all kinds. Every national military involvement from the American Revolution to the war in Vietnam has been publicly resisted by some American Christians. Christian conscientious objection and civil disobedience have occurred whenever social, political, and economic issues have had a bearing on religious convictions and practices.

In matters seemingly related only to religious beliefs, Christian groups with a strong sense of their distinctive convictions occasionally have conflicted with the civil law. Christian Scientists, for example, are among several groups that reject medical treatment on theological grounds. The question of responsibility for life, especially in cases where parents have prevented their ill child from receiving medical help and the child subsequently died, has resulted in religious conflict with the civil law. Similarly, in recent years, fluoridation of a city's water for purposes of dental health has caused dissent by religious groups that reject such medical impositions on citizens. Matters of health and medicine where religious freedom and social responsibility clash have been a particularly difficult constitutional problem for courts of law.

More often than not, the courts of law have protected religious freedom in public conflict situations. The Jehovah's Witnesses consistently have expressed their dissent through legal channels. Even as the movement has become more adamant in its antiworldly identity it has sought relief from organized hostility through "worldly" public court actions. Jehovah's Witnesses have refused to salute the American flag because of their conviction that to do so would be idolatrous worship of nation and images. For this refusal they suffered abuse by American zealots who considered dissenting from flag salutes a sign of weak patriotism. But in this and other instances of public conflict they have won favorable court decisions and, consequently, legal protection of their religious freedom. They have solidified their identity as Christians and as Americans, therefore, by means of public dissent.

Where is the line drawn between religious freedom and responsible citizenship? The question is answered differently in the uniqueness of each new historical conflict. In America the free exercise of religion generally has been considered a mark of good citizenship. But religious convictions frequently have clashed not only with prevailing social customs but also with civil laws. To be a Christian and an American then involves tension and contradiction, which gives rise to religious dissent. When this happens, private religion becomes public, religious freedom is tested anew, and religious pluralism proliferates.

The roots of American religious dissent go deep. Puritans in England had contended against civil "Acts of Uniformity" in church matters. They came to the New World determined to implement alternative religious practices. But their attempts to reform church and society also brought out

their own strain of rigid authoritarianism. When
the Massachusetts Bay Congregationalist leaders
tried to enforce their "New England Way" exclusively on all people, for example, the nonconformists among them rebelled.

The early records are full of incidents in which
such persons as Roger Williams and Anne Hutch-
inson rebelled against the standing religious order
on the basis of their own theological convictions.
They were punished according to their persist-
ence, and some finally were banished from the
colony by civil court ruling. The banished dissenters, however, in their turn could reject persons
who verged in other religious directions. Hence
very early, Christians assumed their roles in the
perpetual clashing of nonconformists and the constant springing up of new reform movements
which would become part of the American experience.

Throughout American history, dissent has been
a major religious outlet and focus of Christian identity. Dissent has cracked the cement of religious
uniformity at its most oppressive joints. But religious dissent also has made its impact on the larger
social order. As dissenters, often in the cause of
human justice, Christians have joined together
their dual quests for religious and civil identity.

The rise of the American Protestant social gospel during the last decades of the nineteenth century represented a dissenting Christian response
to the urban-industrial revolution. Masses of pov-
erty-stricken immigrants suffered wretched living
and working conditions. The traditional denominations were largely out of touch with these people. The pews and collection plates of large urban

Protestant churches had been filled by the privileged classes who benefited materially in a corrupt and unjust social economy. The churches therefore were part of the *status quo* whose vested interests contributed to the oppression of the laboring classes.

Furthermore, the dominant Protestant mission ethic dwelt upon saving individual souls without much regard for the complex social environment surrounding persons. Consequently most of the churches lacked motivation and power to challenge the forces of oppression with which they were becoming identified.

Social gospel advocates dissented both from the existing social conditions and from the churches' individualistic concept of Christian mission. They tried to involve churches in programs of social reform and reconstruction, and they reformulated traditional theology with a social dimension. They dissented as Christians, therefore, both from dominant church life and thought and from the existing social structures and ideology which brought so much grief to the American working people.

The social gospel, however, was primarily a white male-oriented movement. It concentrated on economic reforms that might bring relief to laborers in American urban centers. Almost no attention was given to the struggles of racial minorities and of women for social, political, economic, and religious equality. Yet black Christians and Christian feminists have been unusually persistent dissenters from *status quo* conditions in churches and society alike where their religious and civil identities have been at stake.

BLACK CHRISTIAN DISSENT

In the previous chapter we examined the black American religious subculture with churches at the center. We now are concerned with the role of the black churches in the long history of black dissent in America. Out of the black churches has come much of the inspiration and support for the long struggle for black civil rights in America.

Black religious dissent found early expression in the slaves' secret meetings for worship and fellowship. They resisted the attempts of the white slave masters to deprive black people of their African cultural heritage. Theologically they rejected the white Christian interpretation of the doctrine of original sin as a rationale for the predicament of the slaves. Nor did they accept the white preachers' admonitions to slaves to accept their enslaved position in life as providential. To the contrary, they understood providence as the realm within which their liberation was promised.

From the beginning, Christian slaves found Biblical inspiration to resist as well as to submit to their slave conditions. They looked for a new Moses to lead them into freedom, and it was not uncommon that a slave revolt leader envisaged himself as that new black Moses. The most famous slave insurrection came in 1831 under the leadership of Nat Turner. Turner conceived of the event as a modern-day Mosaic liberation of God's oppressed people. But it was the black preacher who provided consistent, day-by-day leadership in black dissent from oppression. If in the extreme "the black church became the home base for revolution," that was because consistently "the black preacher taught his people to look to the future, to visualize a new day."[2]

The new day seemed imminent with the outbreak of the Civil War. Black preachers announced God's breakthrough into history. They quoted Exodus 3:7:

> I have surely seen the afflictions of my people. I have heard their cry by reason of their taskmasters. I have come down to deliver them. . . . I have surely visited them and will bring them up out of their afflictions.

Then, the black preacher applied the Biblical imagery to the present experience of his people:

> The God of battles is leading on the armies of the free, and breaking, with His strong right hand, the bonds of the oppressed. . . . The Dread Avenger is raining down his wrath on the despot. The death knell of slavery has sounded. At the first shots of the war, the captives shouted "He is coming—our deliverer, he is coming."[3]

Yet the new day remained largely a future hope. Some have castigated black preachers who accommodated to the white racist society in which segregation and discrimination prevailed after the Civil War. Preachers did consistently help to provide in their churches a refuge from oppression of their people in the world outside. But in general they had little choice if black people were to survive. The genius of the black church was its ability to retain a sense of hope for liberation while avoiding genocide.

After the Civil War, some black churches developed into centers of advocacy and action for black civil rights in America. Black preachers became civil rights leaders and, when feasible, the locus of political power. Never did the black churches abandon the "holy cause" of black civil rights. Their theology of deliverance from oppression permeated preaching and singing, and their authority within the black community was brought to bear on specific social issues.

In late-nineteenth-century California, for example, black clergy helped make their churches the foci of political organizing for such black civil rights as the right to vote, the right to receive public education, and the right to enjoy full equality in courts of law. "Thus the black clergy," writes one historian of the period, "were to be found in every phase and on every level of the struggle for the civil rights of black Californians, acting as men whose innate proclivity for freedom was enlightened and elucidated in its encounter with their Christian faith."[4]

Black civil rights, however, have come slowly in America. By the start of the twentieth century little real progress had been made. In fact, there were major setbacks as the segregation and discrimination of black people received official sanction by actions of Congress and the Supreme Court. In this context many black Christians had come to accept political inequality and social segregation as "the American way." To varying degrees they agreed with Booker T. Washington's conception of the gradual advancement of their race in America through the personal achievements of black persons.[5] This position resembled

the dominant evangelical Protestant belief that social reform is achieved gradually through the ex-
ceptional moral efforts of individuals performing
their civil occupations within the existing social
order. But the odds were against black persons
achieving success in white America. With few exceptions, only in their churches did they find a
means of expressing their talents and their natural
pride of race within a society of white supremacy.

Increasingly, however, as the twentieth century
wore on and civil rights did not come even gradually, black Christian dissent assumed a more aggressive posture. In 1909 under the leadership of
W. E. B. Du Bois, the National Association for the
Advancement of Colored People (NAACP) was
formed along with its magazine, *The Crisis*. Soon
the world war brought increasing numbers of
black persons into urban-industrial locations as
well as to the European battlefields. During the
1920's and 1930's the NAACP received black
church leadership support as it fought in courts of
law for black civil rights. Eventually black Christians entered the political arena. An outstanding
example was Adam Clayton Powell, Jr. During his
ministry in Harlem's Abyssinian Baptist Church
(1937–1960), Powell served first on the New York
City Council and, beginning in 1944, in Congress.
Meanwhile the Congress on Racial Equality was
organized in 1943 as black Americans again served
in military combat and in wartime industries at
home.

In 1949, President Truman integrated the
armed forces and federal service, thereby revers-
ing the action of President Wilson in 1913. This

action signified a new stage in the struggle of black Americans for social equality with a focus on integration. With the 1954 Supreme Court decision calling for the desegration of public schools, civil rights through racial integration defined the movement throughout the next decade. It was during this period that the modern-day social gospel prophet Martin Luther King, Jr., demonstrated in his own leadership the fusion of the black churches with the civil rights movement. As preacher and as social organizer, King combined nonviolent civil disobedience and passive resistance into a powerful method of Christian dissent. His influence weighed heavily in such groups as the Southern Christian Leadership Conference (of which he was the first president, in 1957) and the Student Nonviolent Coordinating Committee.

The assassination of Martin Luther King, Jr., in 1967 marked a turning point in the black civil rights movement. For those who identified with nonviolence, King's death represented the ultimate sacrifice. But others concluded from this tragic event that nonviolence had failed. Furthermore, they argued that integration on white terms alone endangered the integrity of black identity. In the years to follow, therefore, violence would match violence, and new forms of black- as well as white-initiated segregation would counter gains that had been made toward racial integration. Black Christian dissent became more militant.

The black churches remained an integral part of the new diversity within the movement. In some ways churches intensified the diversity; in other ways churches provided spiritual unity to the movement as a whole. On July 31, 1966, the National Committee of Negro Churchmen issued a statement supporting what then was a controversial movement of "black power." Noting that the "power of white men is corrupted because it meets little meaningful resistance from Negroes to temper it and keep white men from aping God," the statement presented black power as a necessary conception of Christian dissent. Black power meant power and freedom, power and love, power and justice, and power and truth.[6]

The church penetrated the cutting edges of black identity in America during the early 1970's. Some theologians emphasized a radical version of God's special concern for black people, picturing Jesus as a revolutionary black messiah. Others set forth programs of black process theology, black theology of hope, and black liberation theology. Tying these together was the common celebration of blackness in which the union of Christian identity and black identity provided a context for black Christians to express their sense of American identity.

Most forms of black dissent could find inspiration in precedents deeply rooted in Afro-American history. The black churches always had facilitated both accommodation to and rebellion against oppressive conditions in America. Black Christian identity focused on moving toward that "new day" for God's people. From his cell in the Birmingham, Alabama, city jail in April of 1963, Martin Luther King, Jr., expressed the dissenting Christian hope of black people throughout their American experience: "In some not too distant to-

morrow the radiant stars of love and brotherhood
will shine over our great nation with all of their
scintillating beauty."[7]

CHRISTIAN FEMINIST DISSENT

In 1865 the African Methodist Episcopal pastor
J. J. Moore lectured on "The Rights of the Colored
Man in the United States, as a Man, a Citizen, a
Race, and a Christian."[8] Sojourner Truth might
well have dissented from this lecture on the basis
of its terminology and the implications thereof.
She was a nineteenth-century black woman who
effectively combined the causes of sexual and racial liberation in America. "There is a great stir
about colored men getting their rights," she declared, "but not a word about colored women
theirs. . . . I want women to have their rights. . . .
I have been forty years a slave and forty years free,
and would be here forty years more to have equal
rights for all."[9]

It now is clear that black women have been almost entirely hidden in American history and especially in American church history. Yet black
women always have been "the very backbone" of
the churches, "the glue that held the churches
together."[10] It is also true that black women generally have been excluded from participation in doctrinal decision-making, from leadership in representative church gatherings on regional and
national levels, and from ordination into the Christian ministry. This discrimination they have
shared with women of all races in most segments
of American church history.

In much the same way as blacks have experienced the white Jesus in a white church preaching an alienating message, a number of women, too, are becoming conscious of the alienation from a masculine God, a masculine Church, and a masculine theology.[11]

The story of women in American religious history can be told in the context of dissent. Restricted from leadership roles in the churches, women have struggled for equality in the religious as well as the civil sphere. For a woman to strive to be a leader usually has meant to be a nonconformist in most religious circles. To be a nonconformist of this type often has entailed moving aggressively into the spotlight of public life. Women's motivation has been their desire for liberation. Their goal has been cultural change toward sexual equality.

Roman Catholic religious orders of women have provided a regularized structure within which women of that tradition could exercise some kinds of formally recognized leadership roles. The first such order in the United States was the Sisters of Charity of St. Joseph, founded early in the nineteenth century by Elizabeth Ann Seton. Others followed, such as the Society of the Sacred Heart and Sisters of the Holy Cross. These orders helped women of special religious inclinations and talents make the transition from European cultural patterns to American church needs. However, ordination and the priestly functions were out of the reach of Catholic women. They could not share in the power and authority of the hierarchy.

Outside of Roman Catholicism, Christian women generally had no traditional channels

through which to exercise religious leadership.
Most Protestant churches in America excluded
women from all church offices until recent years.
Exceptions to this rule emerged primarily in the
early stages of "Spirit-filled" movements, such as
the "New Light" Baptists of the Great Awakening
and the early years of the Methodist movement,
in which women preached. But the "Regular"
Baptists disclaimed the dissenting revivalists,
including the novelty of women preachers. When
Methodism became well organized and enough
ordained clergymen were available, women were
discouraged from preaching.

Quakers, however, who located religious authority in the Spirit more than in the Bible or doctrine or church, allowed women to preach in full
equality with men. Elizabeth Harris and Mary
Fisher, the first two Quaker preachers to visit
America, were banished from mid-seventeenth-
century Boston by the Puritan establishment.
Sophia Hume and Rachel Wilson were famous
eighteenth-century Quaker preachers in America.
But on the whole, before 1800 (and long after) "the
Society of Friends stood alone as a group which
recognized women's leadership as a permanent
and settled rule of action." Throughout the nineteenth century "women with a call to preach were
more often found on the fringes of organized religion, responding to emotional needs not met by
existing institutions."[12]

The dissenting roles of American Christian
women took shape during the first half of the nineteenth century. Women excelled as religious leaders in several ways. One way was to found a new

religious group. Not only was the Shaker movement organized by a woman, Ann Lee, but Shaker theology set forth "Mother Ann" as a feminine manifestation of the masculine Christ of Christian orthodoxy. Although sexual equality generally existed in Shaker communities, the feminine dimension in the movement stood out distinctively when compared to most churches. In somewhat similar fashion Jemima Wilkinson's Christian charismatic leadership as "the public universal friend" led to the founding of a western New York communal experiment called "New Jerusalem."

Spiritual charisma and novel religious forms thus provided unusual outlets for women who confronted barriers within the more traditional churches. Apparently when religious power became controlled in the form of established authority, whether in sacred literature, doctrine, or ecclesiastical office, the roles of women could be limited according to the general cultural mores. Revivalism broke through such traditional barriers, and it is not surprising that here women became powerful leaders. Phoebe Palmer promoted the perfectionist-holiness revival of the 1830's, for example, while Maggie Van Colt and Amanda Smith preached at revival meetings across the country and beyond.

Revivalism and social reform were deeply intertwined in nineteenth-century America. Women asserted their religious leadership qualities outside the churches as reformers as well as preachers. But when they tried to relate their concern for the equality of women to other movements of social reform, they found themselves in the role of dissenters outside as well as within the churches.

A clear example is the antislavery movement. Abolitionists feared for their cause when certain women began joining together the causes of women's rights and antislavery. Many who opposed slavery did not favor granting women equal rights with men. They felt threatened when women organized *as women* to oppose slavery. Others who might have sympathized with women believed that combining the two causes would lose support for antislavery. But there was no stopping some women.

Lucretia Mott, for example, was an outstanding Quaker minister who founded the Philadelphia Female Antislavery Society. More adamant were the Grimke sisters, Angelina and Sarah. In her "Appeal to the Christian Women of the South," Angelina called for an attack on slavery "on Christian ground . . . with Christian weapons." Sarah stated more directly that "the rights of women, like the rights of slaves, need only be examined to be understood and asserted."[13] Though not specifically feminist in appeal, it nevertheless was significant that the most dynamic literary force in the antislavery cause, *Uncle Tom's Cabin* (1851–1852), was written by a woman, Harriet Beecher Stowe. Above all, it was Sojourner Truth who personified the combination of racial and sexual oppression as a dissenting victim.

It was not long in the nineteenth century before Christian feminists began pioneering in a more academic assertion of their rights as women. Theological training for women proved to be a difficult but productive battleground. In 1821 Emma Willard broke tradition by founding a "female seminary" in Troy, New York. Fifteen years later (1836) Mary Lyon founded Mount Holyoke Seminary for women. But it was not until mid-century that Antoinette Brown Blackwell made her way through theological studies at Oberlin College against all persuasive efforts of her teachers and colleagues. She became the first woman ordained into the Congregational ministry.

Within most Protestant denominations women suffered restrictions from religious leadership by male-dominated power structures. Mission programs brought these restrictions to a head. Mission societies commonly did not appoint women to the mission fields unless they were accompanied by their husbands. Single women had no place. Consequently women organized their own mission societies—societies of missionary dissent—and appointed their own women missionaries. Through these alternative societies, perhaps more than in any other single way, women were able to emerge as affective leaders in the mainline Protestant denominations.

Although the Protestant women's mission societies fulfilled some of the functions of Catholic orders for women, the two differed in crucial ways. As highly organized voluntary movements, the societies provided spontaneous power bases for all kinds of laywomen. They were relatively autonomous within the denominations. Catholic religious orders, in contrast, were highly restricted within the church. Eventually, when Catholic laity began to organize religious societies, Catholic women dissented from male domination just as did Protes-

tant women. It is not surprising that in 1912 the
first local Federation of Catholic Women was
founded in St. Tammany County, Louisiana, just as
the male-dominated American Federation of
Catholic Societies reached its height of activity.

After the Civil War, pulpits and platforms generally remained closed to women. Churchmen,
though outnumbered by churchwomen, maintained exclusive clerical control on what they considered to be natural, cultural, logical, Biblical, and
theological grounds. During the height of the political suffrage movement, when women also tried to
gain a greater voice in church life, clerical debates
over "the woman's place" frequently became emotionally heated. At one New York City Methodist
ministers' meeting in 1877 a bishop went so far as to
declare (for the record) that "if the mother of our
Lord were on earth I should oppose her preaching
here." Against this attitude Christian women argued for their religious equality on Biblical, theological, and American constitutional grounds, determined to upset sexist orthodoxy. "The orthodox
church," wrote one Presbyterian churchwoman in
Chicago, "has been almost suicidal in its treatment
of women."

> Our young women have been denied admittance
> into theological schools; they have been compelled
> to go out into the by-ways and hedges; they have
> been persecuted for righteousness' sake. The
> church has decreed that two-thirds of its members
> shall be governed by the masculine one-third; but
> despite this decision, women will preach and the
> world will listen.[14]

Women did make their voices heard, speaking not only from within their own mission societies but in many "by-ways and hedges." During the late nineteenth and early twentieth centuries, Christian women asserted themselves in a myriad of social reform movements. Frances Willard gave leadership to the Women's Christian Temperance Union. She advocated "that blessed trinity of movements, Prohibition, Woman's Liberation and Labor's uplift."[15]

From outside the churches but influential among Christians, Jane Addams devoted her energies to a plethora of such causes as labor, woman's suffrage, and international peace. For her pacifist stand she took much abuse during World War I. From within the church but influential in wider circles, Dorothy Day worked and wrote distinctively in the Catholic Worker Movement during the great depression of the 1930's.

These are only three examples among many which suggest how women carried social Christianity far beyond the reaches of what was considered church respectability by the majority even of social-minded Christians. The revolutionary implications of woman's suffrage, for example, were too hot to handle for the male leaders of the social gospel who in so many other areas expressed strong dissent against social injustices.

At the same time, new spirit-oriented movements outside the mainline churches continued to provide means by which women could express themselves religiously in the public forum. These movements ranged from Mary Baker Eddy's founding and leadership of Christian Science, to

the Foursquare Gospel Pentecostal preaching of
Aimee Semple McPherson, to Nora Hunter's fifty
years of preaching and missions-organizing in the
Holiness Church of God (Anderson, Indiana).

Finally, a certain kind of scholarly religious dissent was produced by talented American women.
During the last half of the nineteenth century,
women published articles and books in a wide
range of feminist-oriented topics in which religion
figured heavily. Margaret Fuller, America's first
religious (transcendentalist) philosopher of feminism, published her *Women in the Nineteenth
Century* in 1845. Lydia Frances Child's pioneering study in comparative religions, *The Progress of
Religious Ideas Through Successive Ages* (1855),
and Harriet Beecher Stowe's more popular
Women in Sacred History (1873) further extended
the feminist involvement in religious studies. In
1876 a remarkable publishing event occurred.
Julia Evelina Smith's single-handed translation of
the Bible from the original languages into English
appeared on the market. But the high moment in
feminist scholarship of a truly dissenting nature
came in 1895 with Elizabeth Cady Stanton's publication of *The Woman's Bible.*

The Woman's Bible was produced by a revising
committee of twenty-five women who were dissatisfied with the English Revised Version of the
Bible published in 1881–1885. No woman, not
even Julia Evelina Smith, had been asked to participate in that scholarly venture which began in
1870, though there were many women eminently
qualified. The women rebelled. "Whatever the Bible may be made to do in Hebrew or Greek,"

commented Stanton, "in plain English it does not exalt or dignify woman."[16] Using Smith's translation, they prepared *The Woman's Bible* as a commentary on Biblical passages that refer to women and passages in which women glaringly are omitted. It attempted to bring Biblical criticism and religious liberalism to bear on the feminist movement of the day. As such it became a highly controversial document in religious circles, especially among scholars, and consequently a potentially divisive factor in the woman's suffrage movement. To avoid loss of support for religious reasons, the suffrage movement disassociated itself from *The Woman's Bible*. Yet it remains a historical highlight in the religious dimension of the feminist movement in America in the late nineteenth and early twentieth century.

Before women won the vote in America, Elizabeth Cady Stanton raised a delicate question. "Why," she asked, "should American women, denied all their political rights, obey laws to which they have never given their consent, either by proxy or in person?" Could churchwomen separate this question of civil obedience from the question of religious obedience?

> Women have had no voice in the canon law, the catechisms, the church creeds and discipline, and why should they obey the behests of a strictly masculine religion, that places the sex at a disadvantage in all life's emergencies?[17]

Clearly at this time Christian feminist dissent had revolutionary implications for church and state alike.

In recent years the feminist movement has been recovering past achievements in Christian dissent and has broken new ground through church-related women's organizations on local, regional, and national levels. Church Women United has organized a major interdenominational effort, for example. Moreover, the implications of various modes of feminist theology are extremely far-reaching in American Christian life and thought: "Feminist theologians are not reformers but revolutionaries."[18] Christian advocates of women's liberation have moved in new ways beyond quiet dissatisfaction into the arena of dissent. Historically, countless women have served quietly in secondary church roles. Their identities remain unfortunately anonymous. Alongside them, feminist voices and activities of dissent from "the woman's place" in church and society have made a profound impact in America. Today a veritable renaissance of feminist Christian dissent has arrived.

FOREIGN CHRISTIAN DISSENT

Christian feminists and black Christians are two major kinds of examples of Americans whose quest for identity has led them into patterns of religious dissent. Immigrant churches have expressed a third kind of dissent in their resistance to the complete Americanization of their religion. Dubbed as "foreigners in our midst" by native-born Americans, many developed their sense of identity in America in part as Christian dissenters.

Old and New World traditions clashed ever

anew as recent immigrants made their presence felt within the older American denominational churches. Foreign-language (non-English)
churches within the large Protestant denominations as well as within Roman Catholicism helped
preserve the immigrants' distinctive theology,
worship, and customs. Many of these eventually
became fully assimilated into the older American
churches. Others have maintained some of their
ethnic characteristics. In recent years the influx of
Spanish-speaking people and Asian people has resulted in a confrontation of Third World Christian
identity with the combination of Old World (European) and New World Christian identity in America. Puerto Rican and Chicano immigrants have
asserted their concerns especially within American Roman Catholicism, and Asian-American cau-
cuses have been organized within some Protestant
denominations.

Immigrants also resisted the pressures of Americanization in their religious life by remaining outside the older American denominations whose
fundamental traditions they shared. They preserved their European national identities in America by forming new "hyphenated-American"
denominations (such as German-Baptists, Italian-
Baptists, Swedish-Baptists, and Norwegian-Bap-
tists). One of the most forceful examples of this
form of dissent from the Americanization of a
European tradition is the Missouri Synod Lutheran Church, founded in 1847. This church has
maintained its distinct identity completely separate from other American Lutherans.

In Chapter 1 we noted that nineteenth-century

immigrant churches helped new Americans make
the transition from their Old to their New World
identity. In subsequent chapters we examined the
processes of religious withdrawal, religious subcultures, and religious dissent as modes of Christian
responses to the American environment of religious freedom and pluralism. In Chapter 4 we
shall describe how certain Christians responded to
their American environment by attempting to
mold the nation into the image of their religion.
They translated European Christendom into visions of a Christian America. It remains for us to
note that some immigrant national state church
traditions held fast to the principle of European
Christendom in America by combining elements
of withdrawal, subculture, and dissent while rejecting the idea of a Christian America in their
quest for Christian identity in America.

These were persons who believed that all of life
must be lived within the context of Christian institutions. Since the United States was a nation with
no state church, its institutions could not be considered Christian. Furthermore, these recent immigrants could not satisfy their deepest convictions in the popular and public forms of American
denominational Christianity. Hence they identified with their European state church traditions
which they carefully distinguished both from the
nation and from American Christianity-in-general.

Nevertheless, they continued to believe that the
church should guide public life. More specifically,
they believed that Christians must be public citizens without sacrificing or compromising what
they considered to be true Christianity. This posi-

tion led them to the dual roles of being responsible public citizens on the one hand and members of a minority subculture Christendom on the other hand. They believed in one true church, which ideally should include all Christians; but in a secular society which allows many churches, at least those persons in the one true church could be public citizens and church members at the same time. The nation itself may not be Christian, but the true church continues to live within the nation encompassing the whole lives of certain of the nation's citizens.

Christians who assumed that the church should be involved in all of life reacted to what they considered secular elements of American society by separating from them as much as possible and instituting their own Christian world within the nation. This process occurred especially where secularized social institutions reached into traditional family and personal life.

A good illustration is education. In this case the Roman Catholic response is the prime example. American Catholics began to develop their parochial schools as a substitute for public education. They felt that public schools were Protestant-oriented. But they were more concerned about the lack of any Christian indoctrination in public schools. Catholics assumed that the education of youth was a sacred process in which Christian instruction was necessary. That public schools in an increasingly secular society make no provision for Christian instruction may seem natural for most present-day Americans, but for many nineteenth-century Christians this was a drastic situation. For them the Sunday school (itself an innovation appearing first in England) could not balance a full week of secular public education.

Roman Catholics were not alone in this concern about Christian education. Some Protestant immigrant churches went to great extremes trying to institutionalize a Christian subculture in America. An example is the Christian Reformed Church during the early years of the twentieth century. Here was a small Christian community of Dutch immigrants who had broken away from the larger Reformed Church in America in the middle of the nineteenth century. Their motive was to declare their independence from all American Protestant denominations and to preserve what they considered to be pure Reformed tradition. Their first seventy-five years of life in the New World was marked by the large tensions of becoming assimilated into American life. How could they become fully American citizens without losing their cultural-religious souls? They struggled in every aspect of their life to preserve their separate identity while becoming integrated into American life. They had a strong sense of responsibility, theologically grounded, to be involved constructively in the social order as Christian citizens.

So they lived with this tension of Christian separatism and civic involvement on Christian principles. They debated over whether to support public schools or develop their own private schools. They reasoned that public schools "had to be indifferent to religion and the church, and therefore [public schools] could in effect only silence true Christianity."[19] But this tension was more dramatically expressed in their direct involvements in American political life. Believing that Christians should not identify with non-Christians or even with non-Calvinist Christians in public institutions, they formed Calvinistic Christian political parties within which to identify as a Christian political force in America. Likewise they formed Christian labor unions to function alongside, but not interact with, the large secular labor organizations in America.

Here was a Christian church trying to remain pure in its heritage by separating from the mainstream of American public institutions. While it did not thoroughly withdraw from public life, it followed an aggressively separatist and to some extent dissenting public program identified clearly as Christian.

In the final analysis, all forms of Christianity are to some extent estranged from American cultural forces. Just as Christianity cannot exist as an abstraction apart from some specific cultural expression, so it cannot be totally identified with any single culture. Christianity is a world religion which lives in many different cultures, but is bound to none. Nevertheless, in America certain groups of Christians have been particularly estranged from the dominant cultural life of the nation. For them to become publicly visible has meant bearing the burden of nonconformity.

The other extreme has thrived no less powerfully in America. Some Christians have located much of their religious identity in the nation itself. When this happens, we cross the line from Christianity *in* the nation to Christianity *of* the nation.

4

American Christendom:
Protestant
and Catholic Aspirations

What does it mean to be an American? Americans have been asking this question since their nation began over two hundred years ago. Their question reaches beyond concern with national power and prestige, though it includes both of these. Their question asks about national identity, which involves the individual's identity as an American citizen.

THE BIRTH OF NATIONAL IDENTITY

The question of national identity has been asked with a sense of urgency partly because America has been a nation in the making. America began at a particular time under certain pressing social, economic, and political circumstances. The nation's "founders" conceived of a new kind of society and created a political structure through which they intended to bring their social conception into a national reality. These founders represented the original first-generation Americans who had to transform their former national identities into a new and developing national identity. Immigrants to America ever since have made this national identity transformation and grappled with the question: What is the meaning of America?

The answers have varied. America has meant many things to many people. At its deepest level, American identity has become mixed with religious identity. Consequently the sense of national identity has varied as widely among Americans as have their religious persuasions. It has not meant the same to be a Christian American, a Jewish American, a Buddhist American, or some other kind of religiously oriented American. Indeed, American Christians have differed widely in their sense both of religious and of national identity.

At the same time, citizens of widely varying religious persuasions have experienced a common sense of sacredness in American civil ideology, institutions, and customs. This "civil religion," or "religion of the Republic," developed its own sacred days, ceremonies, and symbols, its own beliefs and myths. Thanksgiving Day and Memorial Day, Presidential inaugurations, and flag ceremonies preceding sports events are common examples of civil religious practices. On these occasions people have affirmed their identity as "one nation, under God."

Civil religion is not unique to America. Most nations express a religious dimension in their civic life. Civil religion provides a sense of national purpose in human history. It is the way in which citizens ask, and answer, the question: What does it mean to be a Russian, a South African, a Japanese, an Israeli, a Mexican, or an American? It identifies a nation with forces beyond itself, while it also reaffirms the nation's distinctive qualities. It is not nation worship, but the nation's worship.

American civil religion has thrived on a conception of America's providential mission in the world. Citizens of widely varying cultural orientations have believed that American ideals, institutions, and history bear universal truths which apply to all peoples of the world.

These ideas about America's exemplary qualities were rooted, in part, in the mind-set and world view of the age of reason—the age of the enlightenment. In colonial America the spirit of the enlightenment reached its height during the last half of the eighteenth century, when the nation was founded. Some of the nation's most influential political leaders and constitutional theorists were rationalists and deists. They believed that human reason could grasp the harmonious, unchanging, and universal laws of nature. They also believed that human reason could conceive of a society that would be ordered according to these natural laws, and that such a society could be established. This is what they intended to create in America. "When, before the present epocha," wrote John Adams in 1776, "had three millions of people full power and a fair opportunity to form and establish the wisest and happiest government that human wisdom can contrive?"[1]

This "wisest and happiest government" would be a constitutional democracy based on high humanitarian ideals. It would maintain a balance of powers within the government. It would respect individual civil liberties and religious freedom.

But it also would command responsible citizenship in the interests of public law and order. Its legal system would provide equal justice for all citizens. Overall, the ideal of life, liberty, and the pursuit of happiness would be the chief end of government.

These would become elements in the nation's ideology which were assumed to be in accord with human reason and natural law. Therefore America, bearer of universal truth, would be the model for the world and the bright star of the world's destiny.

The idea of "destiny" brought the question of national identity into the realm of history. What is the meaning of America in human history? From the beginning, one answer focused on the timeliness of the new nation. America came into being in "the fulness of time," to use the Biblical image. Variations in this American historical consciousness emerged as the nation's life unfolded in the nineteenth century.

Some experienced as hope the nation primarily oriented toward the future. To them America was a new society, the new beginning for humankind, a break with the Old World in order to start over in the New World. In Emerson's words: "America is a country of the future. . . . It is a country of beginnings, of vast designs, and expectations. It has no past; all has an onward and prospective look."² A half century later Archbishop John Ireland of St. Paul, Minnesota, spoke glowingly of America's destiny.

> The chosen nation of the future! She is before my soul's vision. Giant in stature, comely in feature,

buoyant in the freshness of morning youth, ma-
tronly in prudent stepping, the ethereal breezes of
liberty caressing with loving touch her tresses, she
is (no one seeing her can doubt it) the queen, the
mistress, the teacher of coming ages. To her keeping the Creator has entrusted a mighty continent
... which he had held in reserve for long centuries,
awaiting the propitious moment in humanity's
evolution to bestow it on men when men were
worthy to possess it. . . . Of this nation it is the
mission to give forth a new humanity. She embod-
ies in her life and institutions the hopes, the ambi-
tions, the dreamings of humanity's priests and
prophets. . . . The nation of the future! Need I name
it? . . . It is the United States of America.[3]

Others looked backward. They interpreted as
memory the meaning of America oriented toward
the past. They visualized America recovering the
virtues, while rejecting the corruptions, of a past
golden age. They looked especially to ancient Israel, Greece, and Rome for ethical, cultural, and
political models. The American nation would re-
store the best of these earlier civilizations, bearing
the combination of human achievements whose
high worth had been time-tested. Rabbi Isaac M.
Wise, speaking in 1869, called America "the heir-
ess of the civilized world's blood, experience and
wisdom."[4]

Many Americans, of course, felt basically pres-
ent-oriented. Either they rejected the past and
were wary of the future, or they simply looked
neither backward nor forward beyond their own
life-span. At best, America was a social experiment
born of necessity, which might succeed or fail in

their own generation. Eventually, however, a historical understanding of the nation combining past, present, and future captured the imagination of the public mind. It became popular to view the nation as part of the long development of history, a new stage in the ongoing process of human social life. America was the frontier of Western civilization.

This interpretation of American history permeated the popular and widely influential volumes written by the nineteenth-century historian George Bancroft. In the following words from his "Memorial Address on the Life and Character of Abraham Lincoln" (1866), Bancroft summarized the American saga:

> In the fulness of time a republic rose up in the wilderness of America. Thousands of years had passed away before the child of the ages could be born. From whatever there was good in the systems of former centuries she drew her nourishment; the wrecks of the past were warnings. . . . The fame of this only daughter of freedom went out into all lands of the earth; from her the human race drew new hope.[5]

Lincoln himself had proclaimed this "child of the ages" to be the "last, best hope of earth."[6] The American people could identify with such a national conception, regardless of their differing cultural backgrounds. Indeed, they were building a new kind of society formed out of the nations of the world, a society whose time had come. They were the peoples of the Old World come together in the New World to form a new humanity. This was their mission. To be an American meant identifying with and participating in a historic world mission. They were citizens of a special nation of universal truth and historic destiny.

This theme of national truth and destiny penetrated the American mind and spirit. It is found in much of nineteenth-century American literature. It is found in history books, in public addresses, in government policy statements. It was ingrained in the minds of schoolchildren and preached to immigrants. Above all, this conception of America's providential place in world history became enmeshed in the people's religious traditions. It thereby provided one powerful correlation of a person's national and religious identities.

American civil religion, though independent of all particular churches or synagogues, could be made congenial to their various denominations and traditions. Yet its roots were primarily Judeo-Christian. Especially strong were the Hebrew prophets' ideas of a chosen people in a promised land carrying out a mission of national righteousness as "a light to the nations."

Nineteenth-century American Christians could draw upon a long heritage as they joined together their religious and national identities. One can read the history of colonial America as a series of Christian "holy experiments." The Anglicans at Jamestown, the Roman Catholics in Maryland, the Moravians in Georgia, the Pilgrims on Plymouth Plantation, the Quakers in Pennsylvania, and especially the Puritans in Massachusetts Bay and Connecticut had intended to establish ideal societies based on religious principles. Their political, economic, and religious motives were intertwined. Their visions of a good society contained theological dimensions. God had provided a new land of opportunity. It only remained for a people to seize the opportunity and create a righteous society.

The early New England Puritans consistently articulated their sense of participating in the unfolding of a new Christian civilization. They understood their "errand into the wilderness" to be a historic, divinely ordered mission. As a chosen people in covenant with one another and with God, they would be a new Israel, a "city upon a hill," a righteous society for the world to observe and imitate.[7]

The Puritans' interpretation of their mission in the New World became deeply ingrained in American consciousness. It was most consistently expressed in colonial preaching, especially on occasions of civic importance such as election day sermons. Jonathan Edwards, writing about the revival of Christianity in America in which he was a leading preacher and theologian, declared America to be the soil upon which the Kingdom of God would begin its spread over the world—"the Church's latter-day glory," as he put it. Later, during the nation's infancy, President Ezra Stiles of Yale College preached on "The United States Elevated to Glory and Honor" (1783). He prophesied that the American Republic would "illuminate the world with truth and liberty, as part of God's providential conversion of the world."[8]

Already the historical element in the new nation's identity was becoming interwoven with Christian theological themes. Thomas Brockway of Hartford, for example, in 1784 preached on the meaning of the American Revolution and the future of the nation:

> Empire, learning and religion have in past ages been travelling from East to West, and this continent is their last Western stage; the great Pacific ocean which bounds the Western part of the continent, will bound their further progress in this direction. Here God is erecting a stage on which to exhibit the great things of His Kingdom, the stage is spacious, the territory extensive, such as no other part of the globe can equal; and here from the analogy of reason and providence, we can expect God's greatest works. And no doubt this interesting revolution of American independence is a leading step; the world is far advanced in age, from prophecy it is apparent that when we consider above three thousand miles of Western territory, the most fertile part of America, yet uninhabited: can we not suppose this is the wilderness and the solitary place that shall be glad and the desert that shall bloom as the rose.[9]

In this "analogy of reason and providence," Christian churchmen could relate the covenant theology of their heritage to the social contract philosophy of the enlightenment which had undergirded the Declaration of Independence. They could combine their reason, being in harmony with natural laws, with their belief in divine providence, and thereby find universal truth in the American Constitution. For them the meaning of America harmonized with the truth of Christianity.

This, then, is the kind of thinking we will find

among a large segment of American Christians as we scan the nineteenth century. They believed America to be the providential embodiment of infinite, ultimate values. They believed that Christianity was at the heart of the nation, that America was the primary Christian civilization of the world. They believed that the churches' continuing obedience to their divine mandate to permeate all of the nation's life would be carried through the nation into the world. They therefore expressed a continual sense of urgency, of crisis and opportunity, of the fullness of time in which the Kingdom of God was at hand and they were the chosen instruments in its unfolding.

The Protestant descendants of colonial American Puritanism most readily and thoroughly adopted this national religious consciousness for their own. During the nineteenth century they projected their sense of Christian identity into the nation. The Congregationalists, Unitarians, Presbyterians, Baptists, Quakers, Episcopalians, Methodists, Disciples of Christ, and the many smaller offshoots and relatives of these denominations came to share a sense of embodying and building an American Christian civilization. To this Protestant vision of America we now turn.

THE VISION OF PROTESTANT AMERICA

The prospects for Christianity in America looked dismal to some Protestant church leaders as the nineteenth century began. They feared that without a state-supported church, neither the church nor the state could survive. The social order might be reduced to anarchy, they warned, and the churches would splinter into many ineffective warring sects.

These churchmen were alarmed that only a small proportion of the nation's population were church members, though the majority of church members were Protestants. Even taking account of the fact that the attendance at regular services of worship usually far exceeded the number of actual church members, at least 75 percent of the population were out of touch with church life. Without a state church permeating social institutions, would not the unchurched lose all contact with Christian faith, values, and customs? If so, then America might degenerate into a pagan culture.

To make matters worse, the Revolution further disrupted the parish structures which had been breaking down throughout the eighteenth century. The people were becoming increasingly mobile, moving beyond the reaches of organized religion. Even in older, more stable areas the churches no longer could depend upon tax support or even privileged status in the civil order. The problem, therefore, was how to maintain the influence of the churches in a free, diverse, and mobile society. Even more pressing was the problem of how to reach the unchurched.

Many church leaders, however, remained optimistic. They were determined to build a church-centered society in America, despite new and difficult circumstances. Their question was not, *should* the churches mold the nation into a Christian society, but *how?* They understood religious freedom primarily to mean the opportunity to become a public religious force on the basis of their own merits and persuasive power. If not by coercion, then voluntarily would the American people develop their national Christian identity.

With this outlook, Protestant leaders planned their strategy. They intended to capitalize on the combined resources of their various church traditions by embracing what has become known as the "denominational principle."[10] According to the denominational ideal, members of the various church traditions recognize one another's distinctive expressions of Christianity as variations of essential religious truth. Each denomination maintains the integrity of its organizational structure, its theology or confessional statement, and its form of worship. At the same time, the denominations join together in a common mission to Christianize America.

This denominational outlook was a useful adjustment to the rationalist approach to religion so characteristic of the age of the enlightenment, and to the situation of religious freedom and diversity. Deists had encouraged religious toleration on the principle that all religions contain a common essence that is harmonious with natural human understanding. If this were true, reason dictated that in a religiously free society essential religion would prevail regardless of the peculiarities of particular church traditions. To the extent that Protestants accepted the rationalist view, they could retain their various ecclesiastical identities while expressing together the essential elements of Christianity.

Many American Protestants made this denominational commitment, though they generally limited the range of their denominational recognition to the evangelical churches of Protestant Reformation heritage. On this basis Presbyterian clergyman Robert Baird described "the evangelical churches in America" in his classic history, *Religion in America* (1844).

> But when viewed in relation to the great doctrines which are universally conceded by Protestants to be fundamental and necessary to salvation, then they all form but one body, recognising Christ as their common Head. They then resemble the different parts of a great temple, all constituting but one whole; or the various corps of an army, which, though ranged in various divisions, and each division having an organization perfect in itself, yet form but one great host, and are under the command of one chief.[11]

Leaders of this avowedly united denominational force set about to make good their vision of Protestant America. They began to extend their influence into society at every point—through the voices of government, private and public education, public media, legal structures, and all kinds of institutions making up the fabric of the nation. At the same time they battled against the growth and influence of Roman Catholic Christianity which they called "Romanism." They battled against free thought and anti-Christian propaganda which they called "infidelity." They battled against immorality and lawlessness which they called "barbarism." These forces were depicted as the foremost obstacles to the successful Protestantization of America.

The Protestant program would require aggressive and imaginative organization in a spirit of persistent optimism.It would necessitate maintaining a strong sense of Protestant unity among the denominations; cooperation would be a priority. Finally, Protestant leaders would have to raise money and enlist personnel.

They met these challenges. Laypersons and clergy joined efforts to secure the commitment and financial backing of Protestant citizens. They organized nondenominational societies (unrelated to church structures) for specific goals: the American Bible Society, the Religious Education Society, the Tract Society, the Temperance Society, the Sunday School Society, the Peace Society, the Antislavery Society, and many others. They built churches, colleges, and seminaries across the expanding nation. They engaged in moral and social reforms. They distributed Bibles and religious tracts in seemingly endless supply. They organized and promoted a variety of evangelistic programs, the most spectacular of which were revival meetings in cities and on the frontier. Eventually the particular denominations organized their own agencies for similar kinds of work. Denominational competition increased the Protestant zeal to evangelize America.

With a remarkable outpouring of energy and ingenuity Protestants swept the growing, expanding nation with their forms of Christian life and thought. They infused their religious ideas and customs into the public and common life just at the

most formative stage of the new nation's development. Encouraging the public observance of the
Christian Sabbath and establishing the Christian
framework of public schools were two of their
most persistent endeavors. They greatly influenced the religious flavor of an emerging
American nationalism. Consequently Protestant
Christianity made a deep mark on the nation's ideology, institutions, customs, and historical consciousness.

Within this "united evangelical front" churned
the ingredients of a Protestant empire in America.
By the middle of the nineteenth century we hear
all kinds of public voices declaring America to be
a Christian civilization in the making. That is,
whether they liked it or not, sensitive participants
and observers of the American public life saw the
nation largely dominated by a Protestant spirit, a
Protestant value system, a Protestant religiosity.
America seemed to have substituted a kind of
dominant national religion for a state church by
means of a common-law marriage between Protestantism and Americanism.

Philip Schaff, the German Reformed immigrant
churchman and scholar, stated the situation
clearly. He contrasted the European cultural heritage as fundamentally Roman Catholic with America as essentially Protestant. "Christianity," wrote
Schaff, "as the free expression of personal conviction and of the national character, has even
greater power over the mind, than when enjoined
by civil laws and upheld by police regulations."

This appears practically in the strict observance of
the Sabbath, the countless churches and religious

schools, the zealous support of Bible and Tract societies, of domestic and foreign missions, the numerous revivals, the general attendance on divine worship, and the custom of family devotion—all expressions of the general Christian character of the people, in which the Americans are already in advance of most of the old Christian nations of Europe.[12]

To Philip Schaff, as to many others in America and in Europe, the United States was "the most radically Protestant land" in the world.

The Protestant American mind found vivid expression in the discussions of church mission societies about their reasons for existence. A good example is the American Baptist Home Mission Society whose ideas blended well with Presbyterian, Methodist, Congregationalist, and other denominational siblings. According to these Protestant Americans: "God has raised up this nation to become a beacon-light to the nations of the earth —under His guidance and spirit to become a model of all governments and to give moral and political lessons to the world." They believed that America was "discovered in the morning sun of the Reformation," and was settled by the "spiritual elite of the world," restored "from the control of the Papal church, that it might be intrusted under God to the guardianship of a great, free and Protestant nation." They went further: "Never before were the destinies of all nations so centered, in the providence of God, upon *one* spot and *one* age." This meant that the immigrants flooding into the land had to be Americanized into the Protestant image. Immigrants should be divested of their ethnic distinctions and assimilated to the older stock of Americans "in feeling, in intelligence, in habit, in language, and above all, in religion." This American religion, Baptists believed, contained rules not only for the individual heart but also for every aspect of social life: civil government, business, education, the arts, habits of dress and diet, social relations—everything! For America was to be a Christian civilization.[13]

For persons with these convictions, the Civil War supremely tested the nation's Christian foundation. Could this New World civilization hold together? Could the divisiveness of slavery be overcome? On the issue of slavery the churches themselves were divided. The Protestant empire was in danger of being cut in two. Some opposed slavery as the most apparent contradiction of the ideals of life, liberty, and the pursuit of happiness. Others supported that "peculiar institution" as the necessary cultural context of American social and economic life.

Tragically, Northern and Southern white Protestants disagreed as radically over the slavery issue as did Americans in general. In the Civil War both armies carried the Bible and prayed to God for victory. Yet it is significant that both sides read the *same Bible* and prayed to the *same God* with the *same piety* and the *same basic tradition* of theological understanding. Furthermore, Protestants on both sides could agree with Harriet Beecher Stowe's declaration, in her 1853 "Appeal to the Women of America," that "The Providence of God [had] brought our nation to a crisis of most solemn interest."[14] While their positions on slavery differed, their common certainty of America's Christian calling remained intact. The particular content of Christian moral imperative regarding slavery was in question, not the belief in Christian nationhood.

After the war, Southern white Protestants settled back into their regional subculture. They developed distinctive patterns of church life, piety, and theology which became powerful ingredients in the whole of Southern culture. Though never out of touch with their denominational families nationwide, the Baptists, Methodists, Presbyterians, and other Protestants below the Mason-Dixon line identified themselves distinctively as *Southern*. The label *Southern* contained cultural and religious substance far outweighing the mere geographical reference.

For the next century Southern white Protestantism dominated the region's private and public life to a degree matched only by Puritanism in seventeenth-century New England. Southern Protestants took their religion seriously. "Few societies in modern Christendom," writes a foremost scholar of the South, could "compare with the American South for proportion of religious affiliation or intensity of religious conviction."[15] Southerners passionately buttressed their regional social institutions and cultural life with their religion. But they also identified themselves as Southern white American Protestants whose values, though not shared fully by all Americans, best preserved the essential foundations of the nation.

For Northern Protestants the war's outcome seemed to justify their hold on the nation. The war took on a mythical aura and a Christian theological dimension. Lincoln became a Christ figure who died for the nation's sins—an event that provided the opportunity for national redemption. Lincoln, who was a member of no church but who spoke like a theologian, became canonized as the nation's supreme embodiment of common-law Christianity. Out of the war came the "Battle Hymn of the Republic" in which Christians compared their soldiers' dying "to make men free" with Christ's death "to make men holy."[16]

Before long, some Protestants in post-Civil War America would be declaring their nation a Christian republic *in fact.* They would understand their mission now to be as much a maintenance program as a building project in Christian America. Although the convulsions of urban-industrial revolution would test the Protestant mission anew, many shared the incredible optimism expressed in these words of the popular preacher, Phillips Brooks, of Boston's Trinity Episcopal Church:

> We live in the completest theater of God's work. We are Americans. I do not know how any man can be a Christian and an American and despair. . . . When a man is both a Christian and an American, then he ought absolutely to glow with hope and the enthusiasms of humanity.[17]

Here was self-confident belief in a universal truth of Christian America. Methodist bishop Gilbert Haven, preaching a Civil War sermon, had described America as the "center of the history of the world. . . . To save this land to universal liberty and universal brotherhood, supported by universal law and sanctified by universal piety, is to save

all lands." America would govern the world "not
in the boastful spirit of national pride, but in the
humble spirit of Christian love."[18]

Thirteen years later (1876), among the many
American centennial orations and writings, Lutheran pastor J. G. Butler of the nation's capital
declared that "the world's history furnishes no record like ours, clear and emphatic in all that goes
to make up a Biblical, Christian, Protestant nationality." Butler felt that the Constitution implied a
Christian character of the nation. He fully expected that soon an amendment to the Constitution would be passed specifically saying so (there
was a movement for such an amendment). Noting
that immigration presented the danger of a
heterogeneous character in the population, Butler
called on Christians to preserve their national heritage as churchmen and as citizens. "There is no
inconsistency between the ballot box and the com-
munion table," he reminded his hearers, "not in a
Christian society." He expected those of a later
generation, celebrating the nation's bicentennial
in 1976, to be enjoying the full benefits of a Christian America.[19]

Many Protestants spoke and acted as if they
owned the nation. They made their religion con-
spicuous and widespread in American public life.
Their piety, values, and historical interpretation of
America dominated the power structures and national rhetoric. Theirs was the popular American
Christianity. Its public visibility influenced the
thought and activities of citizens throughout the
nation. Persons who differed from the white Anglo-Saxon male-dominated Protestant image knew

the consistent pressure to conform against their instincts, if possible, or simply accept a secondary status peacefully. Only the minority of citizens most isolated from public life could escape the Protestant atmosphere in nineteenth-century America if they so desired. We have seen in earlier chapters that many dissented from what they experienced as oppressive elements in the Protestant empire. But many more found ways to accommodate to Protestant America.

To many Protestant leaders, nonconformity and dissent in their midst were evils to be checked and sores to be healed for the sake of the eternal souls of persons and the progress of civilization. With the emergence of new urban-industrial frontiers and an increasingly diverse racial, ethnic, and religious population, the Protestant churches prepared to defend their empire with crusading zeal.

The Protestant identification of church and nation reached its apex as the United States developed into an industrial and military world power at the dawn of the twentieth century. Protestants disagreed radically about how the churches should respond to the social upheavals of the urban-industrial revolution which was transforming the nation. The social gospel called for Christian involvement in social reconstruction, while the majority of Protestants aligned themselves with forces preserving the existing social and economic structures. Likewise the rise of theological liberalism had become a divisive force among Protestants. Yet regardless of their differing social and theological positions, Protestants overwhelmingly agreed that they bore the nation's destiny as a Christian civilization. Protestants had won America, they believed, and now they were challenged to defend their victory. "Nothing but Christianity as incarnated in American Protestantism," wrote a missions magazine editor, "can preserve America's free institutions."[20]

Confident of their national mission, Protestants joined forces in a new series of nondenominational movements: the Student Volunteer Movement, the Laymen's Missionary Movement, the Men and Religion Forward Movement, and the Missionary Education Movement. Likewise the denominations entered into federations for united action: the Foreign Missions Conference of North America, the Federation of Women's Boards of Foreign Missions, the Home Missions Council, the Council of Women for Home Missions, the Council of Church Boards of Education, the Sunday School Council, and finally in 1908 the Federal Council of the Churches of Christ in America.

By the turn of the century, a new Protestant phalanx was on the march to fight for the Christian conquest of America, and of the world. The mission focused on the world coming into America through immigration, and on America going out into the world with economic and military power. Immigrants should be Americanized into a Protestant image, for the salvation of the nation as well as of the immigrants' souls. Christian motives and values should be applied to America's international relations. Home missions would relate to the domestic scene, while foreign missions would carry the gospel into the world and Christianize American foreign policies and activities. Nation and church would be complementary forces in the world's Christianization.

So it was that the nation entered into its first two modern military adventures on foreign soil—first the Spanish-American War and then World War I. Protestants again would compare their dying "to make men free" with Christ's dying "to make men holy." Although Protestant leaders differed in their judgment about the government's decision to enter the Spanish-American War, the majority were prepared to interpret their nation's victory as providential. In his 1898 Thanksgiving Day sermon, Walter Rauschenbusch told his Rochester, New York, congregation that during the war God and Americans were on the same side, the people experiencing "a deep sense of destiny, of a mission laid upon [them] by the Ruler of history."[21]

According to Congregationalist home missions and social gospel spokesman Josiah Strong, in his turn-of-the-century book entitled *Expansion Under New World Conditions,* "it [was] a time to dismiss 'the craven fear of being great,' to recognize the place in the world which God [had] given us, and to accept the responsibilities which it [developed] upon us in behalf of Christian civilization." Had not the American victory in the war against Spain, plus the energy with which Protestant churches carried on their mission programs, demonstrated the truth of his words written just fifteen years earlier in his popular book, *Our Country*? He had foreseen the fullness of time for Protestant America in these words:

There are certain great focal points of history toward which the lines of past progress have converged, and from which have radiated the molding influences of the future. Such was the Incarnation, such was the German Reformation of the sixteenth century, and such are the closing years of the nineteenth century, second in importance to that only which must always remain first; viz., the birth of Christ.[22]

Jonathan Edwards' eighteenth-century millennial vision thus had become translated and transformed in the minds of certain of his nineteenth-century descendants.

John R. Mott was a Methodist layman who more than any other person held the respect of Protestant Americans within all denominations as their foreign missions spokesman and American Christian world statesman. He agreed with Josiah Strong that the world was ripe for America's Christian leadership. The doors were open, and the world was "plastic"—ready to be molded. Furthermore, wrote Mott on the eve of World War I, the United States is "Christian in its foundation, Christian in its traditions, Christian in its strongest elements, Christian in its predominant sentiment and aspirations."[23]

Mott only voiced the beliefs of many political and religious leaders as America prepared to face the trauma of World War I. The nation would fight this last great battle, they thought, as a righteous Christian people. They would emerge from this war thinking, for a while, that the last great battle was won, that the world now was prepared to receive American Christian democracy. So spoke the Baptist president of the University of Chicago in 1919:

> Never since the days of Paul has a universal religion seemed so within the range of practical possibilities as it does today. All barriers are down. All doors are open. All religions are in the melting pot. All systems are being tried by the best of their effects. If, as we believe, Christianity is adapted to the whole human race, if it can solve the perplexities, meet the needs, and promote the welfare of all nations, now is the opportunity of its adherents as never before to prove this and to win their way among all peoples.[24]

The "we" in this proclamation meant, primarily, Protestant Americans—the prime example of Christians *of* the nation.

VISIONS OF CATHOLIC AMERICA

If Protestants dreamed of a Christian America, they had nightmares about the possibility of a Catholic America. They had inherited a fear and dislike of the episcopal hierarchy whose top authority rested in Rome. They believed that the Roman papacy wielded political as well as spiritual power over Catholics the world over. They assumed that Catholic strength in America would undermine both religious freedom and democratic institutions. Not only did they abhor Roman Catholicism religiously, but they looked with horror upon any possibility of a Catholic America.

Protestant-Catholic hostilities in pre-Civil War

America had been deep and at times violent. On
the whole, neither side lost much love for the
other. But with greater power and prestige, Protestants had developed a more extensive tradition
of organized anti-Catholicism than Catholics ever
could muster against Protestants. As long as Catholics represented but a small minority of mainly
British colonial rootage who long since had accommodated quietly to a predominantly Protestant society, they posed no great threat to Protestant
church leaders. But the great immigration of Irish
Catholics after 1820 made the Church of Rome an
increasingly powerful factor in American life. The
Irish not only were Catholics, they also were
"foreigners." Protestants detested the Roman
Catholic Church as the "whore of Babylon" invad-
ing their American "Garden of Eden." The very
presence of "Romanism" in their midst became a
key motivating force in the Protestants' crusade to
Christianize America in their own image.

The triumphalist voice of the Roman papacy
during the second half of the nineteenth century
fanned the flames of American Protestant fears.
Fighting for its political life in Europe, the papacy
made increasingly absolutist claims for the Catholic Church which easily could be interpreted as a
repudiation of a free religious society such as
America. Pope Pius IX, in part reacting to the liberal social and intellectual revolutions of 1848 in
Europe, issued in 1864 the famous Syllabus of Errors which listed eighty propositions to be con-
demned. Among the errors were the propositions
that Protestantism is an acceptable form of Christianity, that church and state should be separated,

and that the civil power should control public education.

Protestants used these kinds of papal pronouncements to support their own case for embodying the true Christian spirit of America. One Methodist author, writing at the time of the 1876 American centennial celebration, expressed the widely held Protestant belief that "the Papacy has a special determination to become master of this Country; and indeed the very existence of that Church in future ages would seem to depend upon such a consummation." He assumed that world Christianity depended upon its prosperity in America (which many Catholics also assumed). Thus he reasoned that the American struggle between Protestants and Catholics would determine the worldwide future of these two powers of Christendom. He forecast the possibility of a religious war in America whose terrors would be more than the world had known.[25]

As Roman Catholic immigrants flooded into America during the late nineteenth and early twentieth centuries, the concern of Protestants about the religious and political future of the nation reached a crisis stage. Typical was the warning and challenge from the American Baptist Home Mission Society in 1889 pitting "North America for Christ" against "North America for Rome."

> But the idea of capturing the United States for the Pope has not for one instant been abandoned. Only the plan has been changed. The immigrant now enters as a factor into the case. From every Papal

country on the globe crowds of Roman Catholics are flocking to our shores. . . . They are held, controlled, wielded and terrorized by the Papal hierarchy. That hierarchy claims this country for the Pope, boasts that he will have it at no distant day, and lays its mammoth plans for its complete subjection to Roman authority. Well, this hierarchy controls this vast immigration, places it where it will do the most good, i.e., where it will best subserve the purposes of Rome; teaches it how to vote, governs its conscience, and superintends its education. . . . They bring a flag blazoned, "North America for Rome." We are deciding whether they shall plant it on Plymouth Rock, hoist it over the Capitol in the District of Columbia . . . , or whether we shall blot out the word "Rome" and put "Christ" in its place.[26]

Not all Protestants felt this threatened by Roman Catholics in their midst. But fear of "Romanism" was deeply ingrained in their church life. As a constant negative symbol in sermons, literature, and church education, Rome represented a basic element in American Protestant identity. To be identified as Protestant meant to be a non-Roman Catholic Christian, or simply to be a true Christian. Consequently when Protestants referred to Christian America they excluded Roman Catholicism, even if they felt no personal prejudice against Roman Catholics.

Zealous anti-Catholicism persisted well into the twentieth century. Though opposed by many prominent Protestant leaders, the American Protective Association kept bigotry alive against Catholics (as well as against Jews and racial minorities). Yet apart from religious bigotry and discrimination, many Protestants correctly expected American Catholics to try to increase their church's public power in America. The very development of an American Catholic identity threatened the Protestant empire.

Roman Catholic identity had been part of American Christianity from the earliest colonial times. European explorers brought the banner of Rome to the Americas prior to the great migrations of British Protestants into New England. Christopher Columbus himself envisaged his voyage as a latter-day Christian crusade to India by a short route, led by divine providence for the benefit of Catholic Spain. According to the best scholarship on the European explorations of America, Columbus helped introduce the strong Christian identity of what became New Spain.

> Columbus believed that God willed him to discover this short route to the Indies, therefore he must succeed; anything else discovered en route should be considered a divine gift to him and to Spain. He daily read the Divine Office like a priest, observed faithfully all church festivals, cultivated the company of ecclesiastics, headed every letter with a little cross, and often concluded with the prayer
>
> > Jesus and Mary
> > Be with us on the way.[27]

In addition to the symbols and acts of piety, the whole structural unity of church and state became part of the Roman Catholic identity of New Spain.

The French colonists in North America also brought with them a strong sense of their Roman

Catholic Christian identity. The real life of Catholicism in New France existed in the Récollets, Jesuits, and other missionary priests. But the French Crown took great pains to establish itself as a powerful Christian force in the New World. Here too, church and state operated together. As in New Spain, church-state conflicts in New France occurred within a fundamental unity of the two realms.

New Spain and New France were both intensely Roman Catholic during the age of the Reformation, yet they did not join together as a united Catholic counterreformation in the New World. Their national rivalry countered their common religious identity. Nevertheless their rivalry was more than matched by their common conflict with Protestant England. England's eventual victory over Spain and France in North America rendered any continuing influence of colonial Spanish or French Catholicism almost nonexistent in the region that became the United States. Yet the British Protestant hostility toward Spanish and French Catholicism would remain a powerful force in America. It would be a factor in the developing sense of Catholic identity in the new nation.

The American nation thus began as a British Protestant-oriented culture. Suspicion and hostility toward Roman Catholics had deep colonial roots in New England. Some respect was awarded to French Catholics during the American Revolution when France became an ally against England. But that respect was temporary. The American Revolution was a British battle primarily, and the new independent nation assumed a predominantly British and Protestant identity.

Not all British colonists had been Protestants, however. Especially in Maryland, but also in other colonies, English Catholics had settled and established churches. They frequently had suffered persecution at the hands of the Protestant majority, but eventually they became generally accepted as a small minority of non-Protestant Britishers who posed no great threat to the colonies. In fact, some Catholics became highly respected landowners and public figures. One of these was Charles Carroll, who signed the Declaration of Indepndence and later held several important state and federal offices.

Charles Carroll on occasion found it necessary to defend his loyalty to American political institutions. This was because many non-Catholics believed that religious uniformity as an authoritarian political force (as in Spain and France) was the inevitable goal of all Roman Catholics. Carroll responded that his "speculative notions on religion" had little to do with his "political principles," and politically he fully embraced the American form of constitutional democracy.[28]

Throughout most of American history, Catholic citizens would have to defend their political loyalty—indeed their patriotism—against accusations that through the Catholic Church, Rome intended to take control of the nation. Nineteenth-century Catholic Americans thus would suffer some handicaps that Protestant Americans generally did not share.

During the early years of the Republic, British-American Catholics tried to keep relatively independent of Rome in all but spiritual matters. This position had helped them adjust successfully to the Protestant-dominated colonies and to identify with the American Revolution. They were reluctant to have Rome appoint an American hierarchy. Certainly the first American bishop would have to come from their British ranks. He did— John Carroll, consecrated Bishop of Baltimore in 1890. Bishop Carroll emphasized the democratic manner in which he had been elected by the American priests and only afterward confirmed by Rome.

Continuing in this "democratic spirit," lay trustees of local churches eventually began attempting to appoint and dismiss their own priests. But at this point democracy clashed with canon law, and Rome intervened at the request of the American bishops. "Trusteeism" was squelched and parishes came under more rigid control of the hierarchy. Especially when trustees appealed to civil courts, Catholic leaders had to confront Protestant cries that the church was an antidemocratic force in America.

Later, the development of parochial schools also became a necessity with mixed blessings for Catholics. Church leaders knew from experience that the "nonsectarian" nature of public schools meant neither nonreligious nor religions of all kinds. It meant a generalized nondenominational form of Protestantism. Catholic schools had to be established if children were to be protected from daily Protestant indoctrination. Yet parochial schools provided ammunition to non-Catholic critics who accused the church of rejecting the chief inculcator and preserver of American values—the public schools.

Lay trusteeism and parochial schools manifested the complex problems confronting the Roman Catholic Church as it tried to adjust to nineteenth-century America. Generalizations about the development of a *Catholic America* are not possible in the same sense that one can describe a *Protestant America.* Catholicism presented no "united front," no Christian empire in America similar to the combined forces of the major Protestant denominations. American Catholicism developed as a conglomeration of immigrant church communities whose ethnic identities clashed. Their only common sense of identity lay in their religious obedience to Rome and their public status of "foreigners." Although often treated as a unity by Protestant Americans, Catholics were greatly diversified. All kinds of Catholics knew that their church was the traditional foe of Protestants, that Protestants largely ruled in America, and that they partly were alienated from society and from the majority of American citizens.

The great Irish immigration made the first major alteration in the makeup of American Catholicism. In 1830 there were roughly 328,000 Catholics in America. In 1860 there were over three million, over half of whom were Irish. During the same period, and throughout the century, hundreds of thousands of German Catholic immigrants arrived on American shores. For decades these two major immigrant groups conflicted within the church, especially within the hierarchy as the church struggled to develop a national organization and become integrated into American society.

Conflicts frequently arose over ethnic differences between clergy and laity. Early in the nineteenth century Bishop John Carroll found it necessary to import French clergy to help provide much-needed leadership in the growing church. But the English and Irish congregations resented this imposition of "foreign" leadership. The problem increased when the Frenchman Ambrose Maréchal became archbishop of Baltimore in 1817. Later in the century, when Irish bishops dominated the hierarchy, German, Italian, and other immigrant congregations objected to being subjected to clerical leadership not of their own kind.

Closely related to tensions among immigrant groups was the problem of developing a united church in the American environment. Catholic leaders disagreed about the extent to which the church should embrace the mind, spirit, and dominant cultural patterns of the American nation. On the one hand, the "Americanization" of Catholic immigrants had to respect their European traditions or they might be lost to the church. On the other hand, not to accommodate European churches to American patterns both hindered the American church's unity and provided evidence for Protestant accusations that Catholicism was incompatible with American institutions.

Americanization pressures were extreme. As the church grew in numbers and in organizational strength, Catholics had to defend their loyalty to America and explain their loyalty to Rome. Catholic leaders differed greatly about the extent to which the church should emphasize the centrality of Rome in its American life. As in most Protestant denominations, there were some who resisted the influence of American culture on their European-oriented religious traditions and practices. Some did not view America as a desirable society for the life of the church. The church, therefore, could best become strong in America only by holding fast to its Old World character. But others were optimistic about America presenting a favorable environment for the growth of Catholic Christianity. The church simply would have to put off some of its archaic European forms, which were nonessential to the faith, and accommodate itself to the American environment.

Hence the complications of being Catholic in Protestant America increased as the Church of Rome grew through immigration during the nineteenth century. Throughout this period Catholic leaders promoted their faith with as much energy and determination as did the Protestants. They forged their way across the expanding frontier. They built churches and schools, established religious orders, and organized a variety of charitable and reform programs. The whole gamut of European Catholicism came alive in America, with some American innovations.

In 1829, Bishop Whitfield of Baltimore, a French-educated Englishman, called the First Provincial Council. Twenty-three years later (1852), the first Plenary Council in America was called in Baltimore by the Irish bishop Francis Patrick Kenrick. During those intervening years the

American Catholic hierarchy had become dominated by powerful Irish bishops: Kenrick of Baltimore, John England of Charleston, Patrick Kelly of
Richmond, and John Hughes of New York. The
Roman Catholic Church had become the largest
single organized religious group in America. Yet it
still was regarded by Rome as a mission church, a
half century away from receiving status as a full-
fledged national church. Many kinds of immigrant
Catholics experienced America from within a minority status. From Rome's perspective they were
missionaries in a Protestant-dominated society.

The Catholic sense of mission in America tran-
scended the church's internal conflicts. However
much Catholic leaders differed in their estimation
of the values of American culture, they agreed that
the best thing that could happen to the nation and
to the church would be the latter's increasing influence on the former. The best America would be
a Catholic America. Some felt that to make America Catholic entailed accommodating the European traditions to the American environment,
while others believed that American culture
should be altered by the impact of European Catholicism. But divided as they were on *how* to
make America Catholic, they agreed on the essential goal. This did not mean papal control of American political institutions. For above all, they insisted that Catholic Christianity in no sense
conflicted with the fundamental nature of American political institutions and ideology.

American Catholic leaders set forth several
themes consistently throughout the nineteenth
century to help clarify the compatibility of their

religious and their national identities.

First, they insisted that the natural law philosophy which informed American social-political ideology had Catholic roots. It could be traced back to high medieval scholasticism. Catholicism not only blended well with American institutions; it contained the supernatural foundation out of which American natural law ideology grew. Roman Catholics therefore could be the most profound Americans of all.

Second, the Catholic Church in America brought together many diverse immigrant groups (a supernatural melting pot). It therefore provided the necessary unity which all societies require to exist in relative peace and order. The church also stimulated a healthy respect for law and authority which is essential to responsible citizenship in a democracy.

Finally, who could argue that Catholics were not among the most staunch of American patriots? They served in wars, obeyed the law, and praised the government. Their political obedience was to America, while their religious obedience was to Rome. The two would not be confused in the manner common to Protestantism. Catholics were the true believers in the separation of church and state. America was the Catholic citizens' nation, but not their object of worship.

For over a century after Alexis de Tocqueville toured the United States beginning in May of 1831, American Catholics have quoted him with regard to the relationship of Catholicism and democracy.

I think that the Catholic religion has erroneously been regarded as the natural enemy of democracy. Among the various sects of Christianity, Catholicism seems to me, on the contrary, to be one of the most favorable to equality of condition among men. In the Catholic Church the religious community is composed of only two elements: the priest and the people. The priest alone rises above the rank of his flock, and all below him are equal.[29]

Tocqueville concluded that the tenets of Roman Catholicism do not necessarily oppose democratic and republican principles. Ironically, American Catholics who earlier had suspected French clergy of bearing a foreign air incompatible with the American church now found an eloquent champion of the church's compatibility with America in this famous Frenchman.

At the time of Tocqueville's visit to America, Bishop John England of Charleston was a highly respected and influential church leader. He staunchly defended the American political system. He also was convinced that the Roman Catholic Church could be fully at home in America and should strive to become a powerful influence in civic life. "There is but one true Church," wrote England in 1826, "and that is the Roman Catholic." He believed that non-Catholic Christian Americans were "not obstinate heretics" but "an enquiring, thinking, reasoning, well-disposed . . . pious people." They would convert to Catholicism if only they could be instructed in the faith and shown the example of the true church at its best. Moreover, the Roman Catholic Church blended perfectly into American constitutional democracy.

Her institutions are eminently republican. Her rul-
ers are chosen by the common consent—her offi-
cers are obliged to account strictly to those over
whom they preside—her guide is a written constitution of higher force than the will of any individual. What call you this? Aristocracy? Monarchy? It
is republicanism.[30]

Another public defender of Catholicism in
America was Archbishop John Hughes of New
York. On many counts he differed from Bishop
England with regard to the American experience.
He rejected much of the American spirit of individualism, self-reliance, faith in human reason as
the guide to popular democracy, and opposition to
traditional authority. Nor was he happy with the
pluralism that religious freedom had inspired in
America. Yet Bishop Hughes defended his American loyalty even as he insisted that the way to save
the nation was to make it Catholic. In America, he
wrote in 1844, "all that is good is due to [Catholic]
Christianity—all that is evil to the perverse exercise of man's free will."[31] It was Protestantism
which had corrupted the unifying power of truth
in Catholic Christianity. Hence it was Catholicism's mission to curb the power of Protestantism in America.

Father Isaac Hecker, founder of the Paulist order in America, was far more enchanted with the
spirit and cultural patterns of the nation. He argued that Catholicism, not Protestantism, actually
upheld the values of human freedom and voluntary respect for authority in a democratic society.
The Catholic Church, therefore, could be recon-
ciled to America, and indeed could fulfill Ameri-

ca's destiny. Consequently he could write in 1859
that "the conversion of the American people to
the Catholic faith was ripened into a conviction
with me which lies beyond the reign of doubt."

> My life, my labours, and my death is [sic] conse-
> crated to it. No other aim as an end outside of my
> own salvation and perfection can occupy my atten-
> tion a moment. But all things in view of this,—art,
> science, literature, etc., etc., enter in as part of the
> means, and command my interest, and demand all
> the encouragement within my reach. In the union
> of Catholic faith and American civilization a new
> birth awaits them all, and a future for the Church
> brighter than any past. That is my "Credo."
>   Individually the faith has been identified with
> American life. Our effort is to identify Catholicity
> with American life in a religious association.[32]

It would be difficult to find a closer parallel to
much Protestant thought about the churches' mission in nineteenth-century America.

During the latter half of the nineteenth century,
American Catholicism continued to grow with the
new immigration. The ethnic diversity of the
church increased as Catholic immigrants arrived
from southern and eastern Europe. Having
achieved a solid national structure, the church
now was better prepared to meet the demands
that immigration made on its ministries. The Catholic Church kept apace in its own program development with the resurgent Protestant crusades of
the age. As Protestants sought to *win* the immigrants, Catholics sought to *hold* them. Many of the
immigrants never had been churched. Here Catholicism held the advantage as the church of the

lower classes, the common laborers, the poor, the "foreigners."

Yet strife between "native stock" Catholics (who now included the Irish) and the newcomer "foreigner" Catholics continued during these years. The hierarchy divided along the lines of so-called "Americanists" who advocated that the church should accommodate to dominant American cultural patterns, and those who were determined to preserve their European traditions.

The most vociferous "Americanists" were James Cardinal Gibbons of Baltimore and Archbishop John Ireland of St. Paul—Irishmen both. Basically they endorsed the optimistic, progressive spirit of America and advocated an increasingly harmonious relationship between Catholics and Protestants. They even suggested relating Catholic parochial schools and public schools so that Catholic children would sit in common classrooms with non-Catholics, receiving only religious instruction by themselves.

The Americanist program was a vision of American unity within which Catholics would blend harmoniously with others, yet without losing their religious devotion to Rome. This vision was clearly described by Bishop John J. Keane, rector of the Catholic University of America. Keane defended the 1893 World's Parliament of Religions held in Chicago as a peculiarly American possibility worthy of Catholic support.

> When we study the map of Europe, we see it split up into tiny divisions. Lines run across these maps in all directions. They indicate not just territorial

divisions; they indicate something more: jealousy, hatred, hostility, divided hearts which are translated by God knows how many armed soldiers into ways of destroying the world. Now, Providence has permitted people from all nations to emigrate to us. This is the privilege that God has conferred upon America—to destroy these traditions of national jealousy that you carry on in Europe, in order to bring them all together in American unity.[33]

No Protestant could have made the case for the Christian democratic melting pot more clearly.

Opponents of the Americanists feared for the integrity of their faith and their Catholic cultural heritage from accommodation to American culture. Yet they defended their loyalty to the nation. They simply believed that the strength of their American citizenship lay in their distinctive Roman Catholic identity and the maintenance and growth of their immigrant churches. That Catholics could be both loyal to Rome religiously and loyal to America politically, most church leaders agreed. They also agreed that America should and eventually would become an increasingly Catholic society.

At annual conventions of the American Federation of Catholic Societies during the early years of the twentieth century, speakers frequently spoke of a Catholic America in the making. One bishop announced in 1902 that "we have a magnificent opportunity here within the United States, we Catholics, Catholic laymen in particular, to infuse Catholic principles, Catholic views, and Catholic opinions upon the public opinion of the people."

In 1911, J. Cavanaugh, president of Notre Dame University, asked if it would be "too much to say that the Catholic Church is a necessity for America, as necessary as the Supreme Court, or the Declaration of Independence, or the Constitution of the United States." Sounding much like a combination of his Protestant contemporaries Josiah Strong and John R. Mott, the Reverend Joseph Koesters told the 1913 Convention of his belief that "America is called by God's providence to take a principle part in Christianizing China, not the shadows of Christianity" (shadows meaning Protestantism).[34] By this time, with the new immigration having greatly increased America's Catholic population, and with the Catholic Church moving rapidly toward a unified national organization, Catholic leaders were beginning to speak with confidence equal to their Protestant counterparts.

> We are Americans, and the day will come when the world will look upon us as "the Americans"; because, safeguarded by our faith, we will have become the real custodians of all our country's glorious ideals.[35]

It now is clear that, historically, Protestants have feared and criticized Catholics for wanting to do what Protestants themselves had done, namely, try to control America's mind and institutions as the dominant religious force. Likewise Catholics have feared and criticized Protestants for accomplishing what Catholics would have done had they had the opportunity. Both traditions wanted a Christian America. They only differed in their understanding of which kind of Christianity should form the American Christendom.

AMERICAN CHRISTENDOM

Protestants and Catholics have understood America in the context of Christendom. They both struggled with the relationship of their nation to the city of God and the city of man. They differed in their evaluation of the medieval European background of the American experience, but their conclusions about the final Christian destiny of America were not altogether different. They agreed that in a truly free religious marketplace, Christianity would be victorious. The question was, which kind of Christianity?

Nineteenth-century Protestants tended to view the great medieval synthesis of religion and culture as the climactic stage of the "dark ages." They emphasized negative aspects of that period when the church was thoroughly integrated into all of cultural life. They envisaged the church hierarchy controlling theology, worship, the arts, politics, economics, even war. Individual freedom, according to their standards, was stifled. True faith lived underground, suffering under the inquisition of a wealthy, corrupt, and worldly church. Only the Reformation and finally the New World democracy liberated the Christian spirit.

By the close of the nineteenth century, American Protestants generally agreed in their understanding of the historical meaning of America. The church provided the key to world history, and church history moved toward an American climax. This historical scheme began with the first westward movement of Christianity as the apostle Paul traveled toward Spain preaching to the Gentiles. Thus Paul integrated the best of Judaism and

Greco-Roman culture into the Christian mission. Then the church continued its westward march into northern Europe and began the long centuries of medieval Christendom. These were the dark ages, but significant because during this time Christianity penetrated the Anglo-Saxon peoples —the culture of destiny.

American Protestants marveled at the providential opening of doors to a new westward movement of Christianity into the New World and a new civilization. The invention of the printing press brought the Bible to the people in their own language. The Protestant Reformation of the church as it broke away from Roman papal control liberated the evangelical spirit of the gospel. The exploration and settling of North America, with Protestant England emerging the victor against Catholic Spain and France, came just as the American nation was prepared to become a free and independent democracy.

Then, looking back over the nation's first century, Protestants rejoiced at how successfully their churches had led the westward march across the American frontier. Churches had been planted everywhere and influenced the public morality as well as penetrated private souls. Immigrants from the world's far corners were being Americanized in the Protestant democratic image—the world being Christianized in America. Now the nation was flexing its muscles as a world power. In concert with Protestant foreign missions, therefore, the nation could continue the westward march into Asia and Africa with a cargo of Christian democracy. Such was the Protestant sense of American religious manifest destiny.

Protestants had formulated their own version of the high medieval synthesis into a kind of American Christendom. They conceived of an American Christian democracy infused by their church traditions. When persuasion failed, they were capable of using force to keep racial, ethnic, sexual, and religious minorities "in their place." Protestant-dominated politics, from fugitive slave laws to know-nothing nativist elections to prohibition legislation, was geared to protect white Anglo-Saxon Protestant civilization. The arts, economics, politics, even war, bore the Protestant imprint. American unity on a certain Protestant basis was an overarching concern, as was well expressed in the following quotation from a Presbyterian publication in 1919:

> If the United States is to be one nation, with common feeling, language, habits, customs and moral and spiritual attitude, the Americanization must center around the largest racial group, the old white stock. Without touching the contentious question whether this stock is the best in the country, even the largest of the other groups is so small compared with the whole that an attempt at ethnic unity about it could only result in failure and permanent disunity. . . . If American life is to have a tone, this tone must come not from the cities with their varied and heterogeneous racial groups, but from the villages and country districts. It is the task of the churches to see that this tone continues one of godliness and patriotism, high ideals and clean living.[36]

Such was the conception of Protestant unity which dominated the thinking of many Americans at the close of World War I. The Protestant Ameri-

can vision, on the popular literary level, can be
seen in another form through the main character
of Charles M. Sheldon's best-selling novel, *In His
Steps: "What Would Jesus Do?"* published first in
1896 and reprinted many times. A sentimental
mixture of all kinds of popular Protestant social
concerns with a widely prevelant piety, this book
focused on a prohibition message. It culminated in
the Reverend Henry Maxwell's vision for America
and the world.

> And the figure of Jesus grew more and more splen-
> did. He stood at the end of a long flight of steps.
> "Yes! Yes! O my Master, has not the time come for
> this dawn of the Millennium of Christian history?
> Oh, break upon the Christendom of this age with
> the light and the truth! Help us to follow Thee all
> the way!"
>
> He rose at last with the awe of one who has
> looked at heavenly things. He felt the human
> forces and the human sins of the world as never
> before. And with a hope that walks hand in hand
> with faith and love, Henry Maxwell, disciple of
> Jesus, laid him down to sleep and dreamed of the
> regeneration of Christendom, and saw in his
> dream a Church of Jesus without spot or wrinkle or
> any such thing, following Him all the way, walking
> obediently in His steps.

The regenerated Christendom would center in
America. In general, Protestants had no geographical focus outside of America—no Rome or Israel.
Though colonial New England may have been im-
printed with "the stamp of Geneva," Calvinist-
rooted (and Lutheran) American Protestants
found no mystical-political symbolism in their Old

World origins in the sense that Catholics looked to
Rome, or even as the Russian Orthodox Christians
in America thought of Moscow. No American Protestant could comprehend, but only fear and abhor
Orestus Brownson's mid-nineteenth-century description of Rome as "every Catholic's native
country or fatherland—the land of his new
birth."[37] Protestants thus could revere their nation's own soil second to none. They were most at
home in New England's "flowering"; or in the
Southern "Bible belt"; or in the "middle section of
[their] common country . . . whereon the great
contract, at [their] period of the world's history
between truth and error, holiness and sin, should
be waged, and the victory won"; or in California as
"a great missionary nursery" (wherein converted
Asians might return home as Christian agents)—
California as "God's instrument in the progression
of his kingdom . . . as a sanctified and hallowed
instrumentality."[38] Hence Protestants, sanctifying
their land and their culture, could closely identify
their Christianity with their citizenship.

Roman Catholics have tended to view the great
medieval synthesis as the "golden age" of Christianity. The church, thoroughly Catholic, penetrated all of life as the civilizing force. It infused
high belief and faith into great cultural achievements. Freedom was known within the context of
spiritual unity—the unity of God made manifest in
the Church of Rome. The disruption of this high
medieval achievement during the successive ages
of Renaissance, Reformation, Enlightenment, and
nineteenth-century social and intellectual revolutions represented historical tragedy. Yet the

strong papal church had kept the true faith alive during times of trial. The separated brethren (Protestants) might yet be persuaded to return. This possibility especially was open in America, where the church thrived in the environment of religious freedom.

The Protestant American synthesis, to Catholic bystanders, was not wrong in principle; rather, it was the wrong synthesis. False Christianity had been infused into public life, which produced a shallow, pragmatic, relativistic, disordered and undisciplined culture.

With the dawn of the twentieth century, Catholic leaders detected a disintegration of the Protestant empire in America. At the same time, the new immigration was adding strength to the Roman Catholic Church in America. During the forty years following World War I, as we shall examine in Chapter 5, Catholic Americans would feel the possibility of taking over where Protestants left off. A unified, neo-scholastic-oriented, politically, socially, and economically astute national church might pull America back together into a unified Christian civilization. Hence Catholicism, finally as much at home in America as were Protestants, might realize their visions of American Christendom.

But no sooner had Catholics come of age in America than they, along with Protestants, would find themselves plunged into a whole new quest for their Christian identity in a post-Christendom environment.

5

Christianity In But Not Of the Nation: Implications of Post-Christendom America

American Christendom has seen its day. Religious pluralism, however, flourishes in America. Christians of all kinds simply are ingredients in the mix. Within the unfolding religious situation of late-twentieth-century America, Christian identity becomes increasingly complex.

POST-CHRISTENDOM AMERICA

In recent years it has become commonplace to describe America as post-Puritan, post-Protestant, and even post-Christian. It is more precise and less confusing to speak of post-Christendom America. This does not mean that Christianity no longer exists in America, or even that all Christians have given up the idea of creating a Christian America. Rather, it means that America no longer can realistically be described as an essentially Protestant nation. Nor has it become a Catholic nation. It is not even an essentially Christian society.

America is post-Protestant. Throughout the colonial period and the first one hundred and fifty

155

years of national life, Protestantism was the over-arching public religious force in the country. It no longer enjoys this position.

America is post-Catholic. For nearly a half century following World War I, the Roman Catholic Church seemed to be replacing Protestantism as the dominant religious force in America. It did not finally reach this position.

America is post-Christian. Judaism and other non-Christian religions have taken a prominent place in society. No religious tradition or group dominates the public order. Therefore religious pluralism reigns victorious over the force of any particular religious tradition. America is post-Christian in the sense that increasingly large segments of public life are void of any religious (certainly Christian) content whatsoever, a process to be understood as secularization.[1]

Historically, the demise of Protestant America can be traced most precisely to the period of World War I and the changing temper of life in the 1920's. The decline, however, can be seen over a much longer range of time before and after the 1920's. Nevertheless, in terms of religious history, a good case can be made that modern America began with World War I.

The United States entered World War I near the war's end, after having denounced it as a messy Old World affair which Americans should try to avoid. Most public Protestant voices in America supported this attitude and called upon America to remain neutral. But in fact the nation expressed greater sympathy with England than with Germany. The large Protestant denominations likewise expressed pro-British attitudes. Old-stock Americans, suspicious of recent European immigrants, still identified themselves as the bearers of white Anglo-Saxon Protestant civilization of British origins.

During the previous thirty years, the Protestant churches had engaged in large crusades for the final Christianization of America and the world. Home and foreign missions prospered, and the social gospel became popular. Church leaders believed they were Americanizing the masses of immigrants who filled the cities. The golden age of Christian democracy was at hand. When the nation finally entered the war in Europe, therefore, Protestants could interpret this event as a virtuous effort by the United States to save Christian civilization.

Nearly all kinds of Americans shared the Protestants' patriotism and certainty of the nation's virtue. They felt their sacred ideals and freedoms threatened. Christian democracy was at stake. But Protestants made it their own religious war. They equated soldiers with missionaries and described this war as the final battle of a Protestant Christian America. Even the long-standing American peace movement adjusted its thinking and activity to projecting "the moral aims of the war," namely, "to save Christian civilization."[2]

Victory crowned their providential aspirations.

After the war, church leaders publicly supported the League of Nations as the world's necessary political instrument of peace. They also launched their own largest of interdenominational crusades (the Interchurch World Movement of

North America) to seal the military victory with a Christian victory. To raise money and personnel, to reorganize their social missions at home and abroad, they marched confidently forward singing as a battle hymn, "Like a mighty army moves the church of God." Their moment of truth had arrived.

Federal prohibition of alcohol following World War I in 1919 increased the certainty of Protestants that America had reached a new high level of Christianization. They believed that alcohol and the saloon had been America's chief domestic evil, the root of many other problems, and the cancer in American social and economic life. Seldom has an issue and a cause united more Christians (including many Catholics) than did the movement for prohibition in America. Here was the supreme example of the churches wielding power as a public force for what they considered to be the moral well-being of the nation. Here, many thought, was public religion at its best around which all kinds of private theological convictions could coalesce. A hundred years of Protestant temperance crusading through literature, meetings, platform speeches, and pulpit sermons finally had come to victory.

It seemed that America, at home and abroad, had won its greatest Christian battles, symbolic of the success of home and foreign missions. But this sense of victory was short-lived. It now is clear, as only was sensed in the 1920's, that Protestant influence in America had reached its pinnacle and, relative to the past, now was to diminish. Many forces and events in American life during the years to follow would demonstrate that the public power of Protestant Christianity increasingly would be shared by other religious groups.

First, torn by political bickering, the United States declined to join the League of Nations, even as the European nations continued to struggle among themselves for political and economic advantage. The war seemed to have made no constructive impact. The Protestant ideal vision of American Christian democracy did not transform the world—perhaps not even America.

Second, the Interchurch World Movement failed miserably to reach its goals. By the middle of 1920 it had totally collapsed. The high hopes and optimistic zeal of its ardent supporters were dashed. The churches emerged deeply in debt and disillusioned.

Third, national Prohibition did not result in tranquillity and uplifted morality in America. Instead, crime increased during the 1920's and social and economic upheavals revealed a society torn asunder. Church leaders lamented that Christian democracy seemed to be failing at home. Their laments increased with the repeal of Prohibition in 1933, an act for which they never forgave President Roosevelt. But already by the mid-1920's some were expressing their sense of spiritual depression for having failed in their national mission.

From the lofty heights of spiritual vision and realization we have been slipping downward at a rapid pace. We are in an hour of spent enthusiasm. Perhaps the greatest disappointment the world has ever known, the deepest depression, is today upon

us. Before two years have gone by, our enthusiasms
have become so dead that even to mention the
glowing ideals for which we fought brings a smile
to men's faces.[3]

But worse was yet to come.

Fourth, the great economic depression of the
1930's challenged the structures of American institutions. The horrors of America in World War II
challenged the very existence of national independence and power in the world. The tensions and
fears of cold war during the 1950's, accompanied
by repressive governmental measures against
communistic tendencies and the clamor to build
bomb shelters in one's backyard challenged the
American ideals of individual rights and of life,
liberty, and the pursuit of happiness. Finally, the
social upheavals of the 1960's in the wake of
American injustices at home and abroad made
glaringly clear that the nation was essentially sick.
America seemed to be moving away from, rather
than toward, the visible kingdom of God envisaged by Protestants of an earlier generation.
But even all of this, alone, would not have clarified
the post-Protestant age in America. Other things
were more directly to the point.

Fifth, therefore, in the 1920's there had burst
open a flood of social and intellectual public criticism of the churches, especially of the Protestant
churches. Journalists such as H. L. Mencken, and
literary artists such as Sinclair Lewis, ridiculed the
clergy and the theology and morality preached
from pulpits. Traditional church leaders lost much
of their public influence and prestige as a revolu-

tion in morals and manners swept through society. Automobiles carried people out into the country-side on weekend holidays and to baseball games on Sunday, away from eleven o'clock Sabbath worship.

In a word, traditional Protestant church religion was losing its popularity. "Organized religion," wrote Methodist leader Halford E. Luccock in 1934, "simply did not register as a field of interest."[4]

During the prosperous 1920's, business and social pleasures captured the imagination and commitment of middle-class Americans who comprised the bulk of Protestant citizens. Recognizing their declining popularity, churches desperately tried to attract the public to their services and social activities in elaborate new buildings. In a business civilization, could not religion be advertised and sold as a valuable commodity?

It finally could not. The religious supply exceeded the demand. Young people no longer flocked to seminaries or to the mission fields. They became skeptical of the churches' role in society at home and abroad. They questioned traditional Christian doctrines in the context of their college philosophy and social science courses. Many examined religion academically in the classroom, but from a distance—"objectively"—as a curiosity, not as a realm of their own personal commitment. During the 1920's American higher education took large strides in the comparative study of religions and in the sociology and psychology of religion. Even seminary scholars concentrated their publishing efforts on such subjects as the nature of religion and the functions of religion in modern society and in the human personality.[5]

In addition to the academic "scientific study of religion," what did interest people about religion in the 1920's was the public display of dissension within Protestantism, popularly labeled the Modernist-Fundamentalist Controversy. The 1925 Scopes trial ("monkey trial") in Dayton, Tennessee, over the teaching of evolution in public schools produced a journalistic heyday wherever newspapers were sold in America. Traditional Protestantism was depicted as anachronistic at best, reactionary ignorance at worst, even though fundamentalism represented only a modest proportion of the Protestant population. Most church members rejected both the fundamentalist and the modernist extremists who battled each other so vehemently. But aside from such spectacular events, the theological and ecclesiastical controversies among Protestants did great damage to the churches internally and in the public view.

Finally, the coming of age of Roman Catholicism, Mormonism, Judaism, and other religious groups as public forces struck the final blow to American Protestant self-assurance. The increasing aggressiveness of Roman Catholics especially alarmed many Protestants. Whereas Protestants had become hopelessly divided, Catholics were experiencing a twentieth-century unity marked by a renaissance in their intellectual and social life. Catholics rediscovered Thomas Aquinas (1225–1274), whose comprehensive scholastic world view offered theological stability in the rapidly changing twentieth-century world. During the years following World War I, Catholic intellectuals expressed their optimism over the Thomistic revival. "The scholastic philosopher may vision a Thomistic thought-empire dominating the Mid-Western desert of Puritanism," wrote one scholar. Another predicted that Thomas Aquinas would "become a fixed American institution." Protestant theologian Walter Marshall Horton, noting that contemporary Protestant theology was unstable in the 1930's, praised Catholicism because "it knows where it stands, and why, and so holds steady in a world that is being shaken to its foundations."[6]

Not only intellectually but also socially, politically, and economically Catholics advanced their corporate position in American life during the years between the two world wars. After World War II, Protestants increasingly expressed their concern about the aggressiveness of the Roman Catholic Church in America. The religious press and the secular press became filled with Protestant laments. Protestants watched church statistics and noticed with alarm the growth of Catholicism. Though Protestants were not actually losing ground numerically, they recognized the increasing public strength of Catholics.[7]

Catholics had learned how to evangelize through public media, and they had made inroads into the Protestant stronghold—rural America. Protestants fretted over Catholic membership on public school boards. The formation of the Association of Catholic Trade Unionists in 1937 caused Protestants to suspect a Catholic take-over of organized labor. Protestants objected strongly to programs of Catholic censorship of literature and motion pictures through such organizations as the Legion of Decency and the National Organization of Decent Literature.[8]

Protestants long had feared Catholic political power in America. They believed that Catholics operated on the principle that "error had no right" and when in power would suppress American freedoms. In 1928 Governor Alfred E. Smith of New York, a Catholic, made a strong run for the American presidency. He faced large Protestant opposition for moral and religious reasons (Smith also favored the repeal of Prohibition). During the New Deal years in the 1930's increasing numbers of Catholics became involved in politics at all levels. President Roosevelt (whom the majority of Northern Protestants opposed in the elections of 1932 and 1936) appointed many Catholics to such influential offices as federal judgeships. Roosevelt's lack of public piety and of moral idealism in his social-economic policy statements seemed to display the loss of Protestant ethos in the nation's highest political circles.

Many Protestants were horrified when in 1939 President Roosevelt sent Myron Taylor as his "personal representative" to the pope in Rome. When in 1946 Taylor was appointed U.S. Ambassador to the Vatican, seven Protestant denominations adopted resolutions calling for the abandonment of U.S.-Vatican relations. During the 1950's, Protestants warned that the "Catholic vote" took orders from the church whose top authority resided outside the nation. Rome thus threatened to undermine the American political system.[9] The culminating blow to Protestants of this mind was the election of Roman Catholic John Kennedy to the American presidency in 1960—an event unthinkable to earlier generations.

Many Protestants believed they were witnessing a revitalized Roman Catholicism making its play for a Christian America. They became uncertain about their own future in America. Would Protestants or Catholics "win the religious race in the United States"?[10]

Catholic leaders deplored the Protestant response to their increasing strength in America. "Once again a crusade is being preached against the Catholic Church in the United States," declared Francis Cardinal Spellman in 1947, "once again the attack is directed against Catholic dogma or practice, not against Catholic clergy but against the Catholic Church as a social institution and a cultural force in the United States."[11] Yet Catholics were in the race, and Protestants felt themselves slipping behind.

We can detect a change in mood and temperament in the public voices of Protestant leaders as the twentieth century unfolds. They developed a defensive attitude unlike the optimistic self-confidence of earlier years. But they did not give up. Both separately and cooperatively the churches maintained vigorous and constructive social activity during the half century after World War I. During the social and economic crises of the 1930's, for example, a variety of nondenominational movements were organized in response: the National Religion and Labor Foundation,the Fellowship of Socialist Christians, the United Christian Council for Democracy, the Fellowship of Southern

Churches, the Fellowship of Reconciliation, the Christian Social Action Movement, the Socialist Ministers Fellowship—to name only a few. Hence Protestants were every bit as active as were Catholics in social concerns, but they were not used to sharing the public spotlight.[12] Nevertheless, nearly every social movement got some nurture from segments of Protestant Christianity.

The segments, however, became exaggerated. Protestants became increasingly divided. Even their cooperative movements and bureaucracies displayed their wide theological divisions. Liberals, including the "neo-orthodox," joined forces in the National (previously Federal) Council of Churches. Conservatives coalesced in such organizations as the National Association of Evangelicals and the American Council of Christian Churches. Eventually some evangelicals reidentified themselves as "Neo-evangelicals," and later others called themselves "new neo-evangelicals," all of which further divided their ranks.

In many ways these competing cooperative organizations canceled out one another's effectiveness and thereby added to overall Protestant disunity and weakness in society. They sometimes seemed to be defensive measures for the survival of various Protestant factions. Moreover, large segments of Protestants were either apathetic or hostile toward large-scale cooperation. Their energies were spent keeping the local congregation afloat.

By mid-century, social scientists and historians were concluding that America no longer belonged to Protestants. But neither Roman Catholicism nor any other single religious tradition would replace "the Protestant establishment." At the least, Protestants, Catholics, and Jews would share in the spiritual guidance of "the American way." Cultural leadership in the nation had become more open than ever before.[13]

Protestants and Catholics alike have struggled with their sense of identity in this new circumstance. Some have maintained the old Christendom vision against all odds. But that position has become less convincing with each passing decade of the twentieth century. Only slowly have Christians begun to realize that the idea of Christianity's "winning America" is based on false assumptions. For no single religious group can win America. There is no religious race with a finish line. America is religiously pluralistic, and Christians are but one of a crowd.

This is what is meant by post-Christendom America: not that Christians do not continue to live, but that they no longer can be identified as *the* normative religious people of America. One perceptive historian has called this development of Protestantism in America "the second disestablishment."[14] For Roman Catholics, no establishment of a Catholic America ever materialized. The nation's religious life moved in other directions.

PLURALISM AND THE PROBLEM OF UNITY

For the past half century much of the most vigorous and rapidly expanding religious life in America has been in groups largely outside the major

historic Christian traditions and churches. Protestants and Catholics of European-rooted heritage
have maintained their relative proportion of the
church-related population since the middle of the
nineteenth century. But many Christian groups
and movements (not always identifying themselves as churches) of more recent origin have
burst forth with vitality: Jehovah's Witnesses, Mormons, Christian Scientists, Pentecostalists, Spiritu-
alists, Occult groups, psychic-oriented groups, and
a variety of radical nondenominational movements of either a fundamentalist-dispensationalist
orientation or a scientological orientation.

Most of these Christian movements have been
developing over the past century. Some originated
in nineteenth-century America. Most of them are
modern American religious expressions of tendencies that always have existed in the history of
Christianity. They are alternatives to the major
church traditions.

Other Christian groups and movements of great
variety originated and thrived during certain periods of the twentieth century and later waned or
died. They are contextual movements of great
popularity but without a sustained historical tradition. Often they last but one generation. During
the depression years of the 1930's, for example,
there was Frank Buchman's Moral Re-Armament
movement among college students, Father
Charles E. Coughlin (the "radio priest") and his
Union Party, Dorothy Day and the Catholic
Worker Movement, the "harmonial" religious
writings of Emmet Fox and E. Stanley Jones which
elicited such a following as to resemble a move-

ment, the "I Am" movement of Guy and Edna
Ballard, and the Father Divine Peace Mission.

Similar lists of popular Christian movements
outside the traditional churches could be men-
tioned with reference to the 1940's, 1950's, and
1960's. In the mid-1970's two movements suggest
how old American themes return in modern versions. The UFO cult represents millennialism for
the space age. Followers of "Him" and "Her"
("The Two" who are considered "at least the
equals of Jesus Christ") leave their homes and
possessions to join in communal anticipation of un-
identified flying objects. These spaceships will
carry away the faithful to God's heavenly kingdom
and eternal salvation.[15]

The Unification Church, led by wealthy South
Korean evangelist Reverend Sun Myung Moon,
draws young people away from their homes into
highly disciplined communities. Reverend Moon's
theology posits him as "the Lord of the Second
Advent," "the completer of man's salvation [as]
the second coming of Christ." Reverend Moon
claims that the Bible is written in a code only he
understands, and that "all Christians in the world
are destined to be absorbed by [his] movement."[16]

For nearly two thousand years particular groups
of Christians have become convinced that the "last
times" were near. Nearly a century and a half ago
some Christians in western New York State left
their worldly goods and occupations to await
Christ's "second coming" as preached by William
Miller and the Millerites. A new denomination, the
Seventh-day Adventists, became one permanent
result of that movement. About the same time,

Joseph Smith claimed to have received a new revelation. Many followed him into a new and permanent denomination. The similarities between the
UFO cult and the Millerites, and between Joseph
Smith and Reverend Moon break down at key
points. But they do suggest the long history of similar types of innovative Christian-oriented movements outside the traditional churches in America.
Today, as in the past, these kinds of movements
have made deep inroads in the churches, often
causing tensions and always increasing religious
pluralism.

Today Christian-oriented movements abound
outside the churches. Millions of persons with no
church relationship (as well as church members)
are drawn to spiritualist, psychic, mystic, and
scientological phenomena. Astrology and the religion of the horoscope also has become popular in
the 1970's. Of more far-reaching significance, non-
Christian and non-Western religions have taken
hold in America. Vedanta, Bahai, and Buddhism
have existed in America for many years. Today
various forms of Buddhism such as Zen, and such
forms of Hindu-oriented faith as Hare Krishna, are
thriving. In other words, religious pluralism in
modern America cuts through traditional Christian communities and moves outside Christianity
itself.

It no longer will do to call these movements and
groups "marginal religions" or religions on the
"fringe." Altogether they represent a phenomenon that may be the key to understanding twentieth-century American religious history. Just as
Puritanism dominated the colonial period and

evangelical Protestantism along with Roman Catholic immigrants swept the nineteenth century, today religious pluralism has come of age and shows no sign of slowing down.

Today religious pluralism is more clearly a powerful factor in public American life than ever before. The communications revolution has made a difference in the public visibility of religious pluralism. Books, newspapers, magazines, records, radio, and above all television present the American public with a full display of religious diversity. The options are constantly before us. Truth claims and religious practices from the world over now are at least as visible as are the traditional churches. The esoteric now is commonplace—no longer esoteric.

Recently an article appeared in the *San Francisco Chronicle* which examined the city's religious pluralism. The "religious smorgasbord" of San Francisco makes this city something of a religious mecca. Actually, most large American cities are like this, and the religious smorgasbord is widely available. Most of the letters to the editor about the article were positive. They felt that the liveliness of religious life (not equated with traditional churches) shows that Americans are seeking and finding a rich variety of avenues to spiritual fulfillment (the fact that San Francisco remains the suicide capital of the nation notwithstanding). Here was a celebration of religious pluralism in a free society.[17]

Is not the pluralism of modern America a new stage in the continuing saga of the revolutionary American religious experiment begun two hundred years ago?

One basic question that first-generation Americans raised two centuries ago has again become critical. This is the question of unity. What holds the nation together? Can a people maintain a common sense of ideals, of values, of cultural identity without a common religious foundation? Especially since the social disruptions of the 1960's, this question has taken on a new urgency. The answer, if there be one, cannot be simple.

Historically one answer has insisted that an enlightened society does not need a common public religion, but is better off freed from religious uniformity. This answer celebrates the American experiment of a free society in which organized religion and government are separated, each to mind its own business without hindrance from the other. Also, in line with Thomas Jefferson's thought, many have assumed that just as the government should protect the churches' freedom to thrive by their own support and persuasive power, so a plurality of religions will help foster good citizens of the state. Furthermore, as this line of thought has developed over the years, certain values, ideals, aspirations, and a sense of American destiny hold the people together, regardless of their many diverse religious persuasions. This is the "civil religion" which in fact has functioned throughout most of American history.

This civil religious commitment of Americans, shared by persons within and outside the churches, centers in the sense that the Federal Constitution guarantees sacred values and ideals of liberty, equality, and justice. Therefore the constitutional democracy itself is a sacred social form valid for all peoples. The nation is responsible to promote these values throughout the world. The idea of a transcendent God in human history, giving special direction to America, has operated powerfully in the American mind—a nonsectarian God whom people worship as they choose, but a God whom all Americans should acknowledge.

It is precisely this aura of American religiosity which exploded during the 1960's. All kinds of Americans discovered that the nation had fallen far short of its ideals and that great divisions among peoples persisted within the society. Historians and social scientists began to dissect the American civil religion. They displayed it, examined it, scrutinized it, and challenged its very essence. Many church leaders separated their traditions from it, while humanitarian secularists called for reform in its name.

Nevertheless, there remains a nucleus of thought, though shaken and though seen to be ambiguous and uncertain, which is grounded in American constitutional principles and which might provide a sense of overall unity in America even if these ideas no longer are held with sacred awe. Life, liberty, and the pursuit of happiness, equal justice and equal opportunity, and the freedoms contained in the Bill of Rights and the Constitution's amendments, still are powerful ideals in American consciousness.

From another perspective, a second historical answer to the question of national unity has pointed to a common cultural rootage in Western civilization which contains the essential spiritual outlook of America. Is not the Judeo-Christian heritage of an ethical, personal monotheism still a kind of theological orthodoxy operating in American life and thought? This answer is precarious, for it is tied in with the forces related to American Christendom.

America has developed primarily as part of the Western world. The dominant cultural heritage has been British and western European, and the primary religious force has been broadly Judeo-Christian. It is a story of conquest. The British came early in the sevententh century and conquered the Spanish, the French, and several native Indian tribes. Slaves were brought in chains from Africa. In 1776 British colonists fought "for their rights as Englishmen" and declared their independence from "the mother country." Throughout the nineteenth century, immigrants came to America from all parts of the world. The cultural establishment into which they were to be Americanized was heavily white Anglo-Saxon Protestant oriented.

But the native American Indian peoples, the African-American people, the Hispanic-American people, and the Asian-American people are examples of notable exceptions to the cultural identity of America rooted in Britain and western Europe. They are minority cultures representing authentic pluralism in America.

The idea of an American "melting pot" of immigrants with a common culture, therefore, has not dealt equal justice to all kinds of Americans. But the melting pot concept might still be useful if it could be broadened. The Eastern religions of Buddhism and Hinduism contain modes of understanding which could harmonize with the idea of a common mixture of all kinds of peoples. Western culture is more individualistic. A combination of the two major traditions might provide for the continuing cultural-religious identity of particular groups of Americans within a fundamental national unity.

In any case, it now is clear that a Western Judeo-Christian melting pot base for American unity no longer will do. The world indeed has come into America, and cultural pluralism qualifies previous conceptions of essential American unity. At the same time, America has expanded economically and politically and militarily everywhere in the world, coming into daily contact with numerous cultures. Today the world is too small and the United States too large for this pluralistic society to find unity in a provincial past. All signs point to a more cosmopolitan future.

Unifying forces in America are tied in with forces of unity throughout the world. But unifying forces may become ominous. Global problems of ecology and hunger plus the power of technocracy (technology and bureaucracy) are common experiences of people everywhere. These are critical problems which transcend national barriers and cultural distinctions.

Technocracy brings increasing uniformity to human social experience. Around the world human technocratic invention is establishing generally uniform modes of transportation, communication media, business operations, manufactured products, machines and appliances, and the interaction of all of these. Furthermore, technocracy in itself is efficient, scientific, pragmatic, and impersonal. It is capable of great creativity or great destruction. It has achieved both. It produces wealth and power, but it does not necessarily make politics and economics sensitive to human needs. It creates common environments for all kinds of peoples, but it does not teach all kinds of peoples how to live together in freedom, justice, and peace.

In other words, technocracy in itself contains no ethical values; it is ethically neutral. Technocracy is totally nonreligious. Technocracy is the energy and substance of secularization. Secularization is neither good nor bad; it simply *is*. Secularization defines much of the common experience of humankind. But secularization does not necessarily unify peoples or make their society creative or destructive.

Only human beings can determine whether secular technocracy will be creative or destructive. Only human beings are concerned with values. Only human beings are religious. Humanity has created technocracy, and humanity must determine how to use its creation. Those who worship technocracy worship a robot god of their own creation which rules without laws or goals. If technocracy is to be a creative force that unifies humankind, it must be guided by humane ethical values. The secular uniformity must be penetrated by the religious pluralism of humankind.

Secularization, therefore, may bring uniformity to the American experience, but it will not necessarily unify the American people. Nor will secularization bring unity to the peoples of the world. As a microcosm of the world's cultures which interact with all nations, America must find its base of unity in humane values within and among the religions of humanity.

REALMS OF CHRISTIAN IDENTITY

The problem of unity in religiously pluralistic America returns us to our primary consideration of Christian identity. I see two main areas within which Christian Americans must come to grips with their sense of identity. These are the *social-ethical* area and the *theological* area. I am going to suggest that the Christian identity crisis in America is analogous to the American identity crisis in the world. In both cases, onetime superpowers will have to lose some of their life in order to gain their souls.

First, consider the social-ethical realm. One of the themes of this book has been the different ways in which religious groups have related to public life in America. In one sense the Federal Constitution privatized all particular religions by separating them from legal involvement in the civil order. But in another sense the Constitution guaranteed the freedom of all religions to express themselves publicly on an equal basis. That is, legally and ideally the government is neutral toward religions. People are free to believe, practice, and propagate whatever faith they choose as long as they respect the rights of others to differ religiously or to reject all religion.

Of course, religious practice must respect the civil laws of the nation. Religious freedom is not unlimited. But this is just where conflict arises, when a person's religious beliefs or practices clash with civil laws and secular practices. American legal history abounds with church-state cases wherein the limits of religious freedom have been tested. In recent years, however, this legal involvement with religion has become increasingly complicated, to the point where the very definition of the word "religion" is uncertain. Some long-standing assumptions are tumbling down.

The situation was simpler as long as the Judeo-Christian heritage provided the religious norms for the nation, and especially when America was viewed as a Protestant society. The point has been made repeatedly by many circles that although church and state are legally separated, religion and public life are not thereby unrelated. During the nineteenth century it was common to describe religion and government as informally and voluntarily interrelated. Early in the twentieth century, people in high places proclaimed America a Christian nation with government deeply rooted in Christian ideals, values, and customs. In 1892, after all, the Supreme Court (ruling on the *Church of the Holy Trinity* v. *United States*) at great lengths described America as a Christian nation.

If we pass beyond these matters to a view of American life as expressed by its laws, its business, its customs, and its society, we find everywhere a clear recognition of the same truth. Among other matters note the following: The form of oath universally prevailing, concluding with an appeal to the Almighty; the custom of opening sessions of all deliberative bodies and most conventions with prayers; the prefatory words of all wills, "In the name of God, amen"; the laws respecting the observance of the Sabbath; with the general cessation of all secular business, and the closing of courts, Legislatures, and other similar public assemblies on that day; the churches and church organizations which abound in every city, town, and hamlet; the multitude of charitable organizations existing everywhere under Christian auspices; the gigantic missionary associations, with general support, and aiming to establish Christian missions in every quarter of the globe. These, and many other matters which might be noticed, add a volume of unofficial declarations to the mass of organic utterances that this is a Christian nation.

Even as late as 1930 the Supreme Court could state that "we are a Christian people, according to one another the equal right of religious freedom, and acknowledging with reverence the duty of obedience to the will of God" *(United States* v. *Macintosh).*[18] But this is the last time the Supreme Court has made such a reference.

Throughout American history there have been movements opposed to Christian privileges and public recognition. During the last quarter of the nineteenth century a National Liberal League and an American Secular Union (merging in 1901) campaigned for the secularization of America and the complete separation of church and state. They strongly opposed a proposed constitutional amendment that would have declared the United States a Christian nation. They opposed church tax exemption, state-supported chaplaincies in public institutions, oaths in civil courts, restrictive Sunday laws, and civil recognition of such religious holidays as Christmas and Easter.

These kinds of church-state concerns could make little headway in America in the late nineteenth and early twentieth century. The power of organized Christianity was too strong. The new immigration included many conservative churches with European-Christendom orientations. In many cases these turned out to be allies with the older American churches' determination to protect the Christian identity of the nation from secular inroads. But in later years, as second- and third-generation immigrants became Americanized and aloof from their European heritages, they also became more relaxed toward religious pluralism and secularization.

During the past half century the old assumptions about Christian America have broken down. The automatic public visibility of Christianity has ended. True, during the 1950's there was a revival of public religion in general, with a flurry of congressional actions putting the word "God" on coins and stamps and into the Pledge of Allegiance. But the reference of this kind of language had become vague, and Christianity enjoyed no priority. Church membership soared, but increasing numbers of these people were almost totally ignorant of anything resembling Christian traditions or beliefs. Then, with the theological and ecclesiastical disruptions of the 1960's, traditional doctrines and religious language lost much of its public (not to mention private) force.

The Supreme Court no longer rules according to Christian norms. Today religion is not even defined as belief in God, but more in terms of the function of sincerely held beliefs. There is neither a conventional model of religious organization (such as churches) nor a proper realm of sacred belief to guide the legal process in response to religious issues in the public order.

The implications of this train of events are becoming visible. Christian privileges in society are being challenged. For example, exemptions from military duty for traditionally recognized clergy, for seminary students, and for such traditionally recognized clergy, for seminary students, and for such traditionally recognized pacifist Christians as Quakers and Mennonites may become no more automatic than for others who claim pacifist convictions without reference to God. The automatic tax exemption of church property is being challenged, especially as the definition of "church" becomes less clear. State-supported chaplaincies in the military, in governmental assemblies, and in prisons are being questioned. Christmas as a public national holiday is under fire. (Some persons are asking that Christ be taken out of the public winter holiday and that Christmas be contained within the churches.) In short, Christian identity in America is becoming increasingly but one religious subculture among many.

As this happens, the tensions that have developed within the churches over the past few decades about Christian involvement in society probably will increase. Many will opt for a purely private Christianity that ignores political, economic, and social problems. This choice will lead

to a Christian identity unrelated to large segments
of people's lives. It will relinquish a Christian sense
of participation in the building of society. As an
identity it will be a private and largely "otherworldly" Christianity neither in most of the world
nor of it. Christians taking this option will acknowledge the primacy of secularism in the world and
in most of their lives.

Others will persist in trying to mold the nation
into a particular image. There still are Protestants
interested in rebuilding the evangelical empire.
There are Catholic bishops today who are trying to
marshal grass-roots support among the forty eight
million American Catholics for a constitutional
amendment prohibiting abortion (Prohibition
revisited?). But the odds are against them. Resistance to Christian moral coercion is strong in America.

Still others will struggle to find ways to involve
themselves and their churches in the problems of
public life. They will do this with a sense of Christian identity working alongside persons of other
religious identities and of no religious identity
whatsoever. They will participate in the public forum with other concerned Americans. Church
lobbies at all levels of government will continue to
plead causes, as is their right. But Christians will
accomplish social betterment primarily by joining
efforts with other individuals and groups that have
common concerns. When these public-oriented
Christians conflict with the majority opinion in social issues, they will maintain their Christian identity as dissenters and accept the consequences.

Christians will not be *the* nation's conscience,
but they will be free to make their input along

with others in the reformation of an American world conscience. Christians will not need to apologize for exercising their voices in public affairs out of their religious convictions. But Christians also must respect the equal right of all kinds of citizens to participate fully, without apology, out of their own religious convictions, as authentic Americans with integrity and value to public life.

Recently the story was publicized that Richard Nixon had considered becoming a Roman Catholic prior to the 1972 presidential campaign because he was convinced that Roman Catholicism had come to represent the "real America." My response to this story (though I was not certain of its truth) was a mixture of humor and despair. Why? Not because of anything to do with Roman Catholicism; but because with reference to religion, above all, there no longer can be such a thing as real Americans as over against others. All kinds of Americans are real, and all religions are equally American in the nation's third century.

In this public sense, the nation transcends any particular religion, recognizing, at the same time, that particular religions may transcend the nation. In both cases the vision is worldwide in scope. This situation, which resembles the situation presented to all Christian groups at the founding of the nation in 1776, does not necessarily diminish but may increase the integrity of each particular religion. The word "denomination" now means not only Protestant groups, not only Christian groups, not only groups within the Judeo-Christian heritage, but all sorts of religious groups. The American Constitution allows each religion to exist solely by

its own internal strength and persuasive powers—
by its own faith and works.

For Christians this situation means, probably
even more than it did in 1776, and perhaps something like it did in the first three centuries A.D.,
religious survival primarily on the basis of an identifiable and vital living faith. According to one contemporary Christian interpreter of the situation,
"Now that the illusions of Judaeo-Christian culture
are passing away, Christians will again become ac-
customed to being a few, tiny remnant, among the
multitudes of persons."[19]

This leads to the second major area within which
Christians must struggle with their sense of identity in America—theological meaning. Here we
are on uncertain ground, but there is no other
ground upon which to stand. A theological earth-
quake has occurred.

The popular religious revival of the 1950's now
can be seen for its limitations. "Religion was in
vogue"; and "America was on a religious kick."
Some popular magazines even described America
as a "profoundly Christian nation." Yet the critics
of this popular "upswing" of religion during the
1950's largely came from Christian circles. They
pointed to the lack of specifically Christian content
in much of popular religion. Certainly the gulf between personal belief and official church dogmas
had widened. The churches were filled with persons ignorant of their own traditions and uninter-
ested in them. If Protestants, Catholics, and Jews
shared the public spotlight, much popular public
theology was not confined to any of these traditions. On the popular level, at a time when Ameri-

can civil religion thrived unnamed and nearly un-
challenged, American religious life was breaking
out of traditional ecclesiastical molds to an unprecedented extent. It was this phenomenon
which Duncan Howlett described perceptively
(though imprecisely) as "The Fourth American
Faith."[20]

Nevertheless, the popular religion of the 1950's,
in retrospect, seems incredibly thin with regard to
theological content or ethical vision. Sentimental
piety and material achievement were its main
characteristics. The "peace of mind" and "positive
thinking" fad played on people's cold war fears
and postdepression hunger for economic security.
The idea of personal and public religious faith in
general harmonized with "flannel suit" conformity and respectable patriotism—manifestations of
a people seeking unity and meaning in a battle-
torn world. The churches did not stimulate much
intellectual and ethical involvement in the really
critical problems of humankind (notable exceptions were academic critics of popular religion).

Consequently for all of the mass-media religious
revivals associated with Billy Graham, Norman
Vincent Peale, and Bishop Fulton J. Sheen, the
Eisenhower years (1952–1960) were marked by
affluence and stability more than by spiritual
creativity. It might have seemed that all was well
on the American Christian front.

Then "all hell broke loose" in the 1960's. American domestic injustices and problematic involvement in Southeast Asia became the context for
social upheavals. The churches became involved
in social movements that tore congregations apart

internally and raised the whole question of their rights and responsibilities in the social order. But just as far-reaching were the upheavals in the broad area of theological understanding, with deep ramifications of theological belief and ethical meaning for Christian identity in America. Not only the theology of American civil religion was shaken; Christian theology likewise exploded.

Protestants, who for several decades had been experiencing a major disruption in their American "synthesis" of theology and national culture, went to the core of their traditional beliefs. There were precedents. Various forms of Protestant theological liberalism long had struggled with scientific advancements and Christian belief prior to World War I. After that war neo-orthodox theologians, the followers of Paul Tillich, and Christian process thinkers for several decades developed systematic theological "schools" of strong academic appeal. But not until the 1960's did some of the implications of these theological developments really begin to reach the masses of Christians who filled the American churches.

After 1960, books that raised questions about the nature and existence of God became popular sellers in America, from Bishop John A. T. Robinson's *Honest to God* (1963) to Thomas Altizer and William Hamilton's *Radical Theology and the Death of God* (1966). Books that challenged the nature of American churches reached a wide audience, such as Peter Berger's *The Noise of Solemn Assemblies* (1961) and Gibson Winter's *The Suburban Captivity of the Churches* (1961). The popular impact of secularization was apparent in such books as Paul van Buren's *The Secular Meaning of the Gospel* (1963) and Harvey Cox's best-selling *The Secular City* (1965). Theological ethics became related to changing social mores in such books as Joseph Fletcher's *Situation Ethics: The New Morality* (1966).

In many ways these books represented a radical departure from the popular religious publications of the 1950's. The theology, ethics, and social involvement of the churches were being scrutinized not only in academic circles but widely among the laity. Yet these spectacular critiques now can be seen also as creative accommodations to the optimism and confidence of Americans generally during the early 1960's. They represented attempts to update Christianity for the times, to make the churches relevant to the age of "new frontiers," to show how being Christian while being American was a salvageable relationship in the 1960's as it had been a romantically euphoric marriage in the 1950's. Christians could join together and with other Americans in building the new society. This was a bold attempt, with commendable motivations and some constructive results, but with some apparent shortcomings.

The new religious books of the early 1960's now read with the romantic aura of America before urban riots marred the beauty of secular cities, before the My Lai massacre and government "dirty tricks" stretched ethics to absurd contextual limits, before unemployment made the Protestant work ethic seem immoral and the theology of leisure seem sadistic, and before many solemn assemblies began either to dry up or to go underground.

Beneath the ethos of early 1960's innocence, however, the new theologies of the period helped pave the way for the truly revolutionary theological developments of the later 1960's and the 1970's. Christian theologians have responded to the explosions of recent years with profound results: radical theology, black theology, theology of hope, feminist theology, and liberation theology. These theological movements are bound to no particular church traditions, but challenge them all. Nor can they be classified simply as liberal or conservative in traditional doctrinal categories. They are theologies of the oppressed, identified with human conditions, providing a possibility of Christian faith immersed in but not bound to the incredible state of the modern world.

This wellspring of diverse theological impulses developing over the past twenty years (the post-World War II era) has struck a Protestant nerve. During the early 1970's, negative reaction to such theological departures began to set in. This reaction took the form of an evangelical upswing within the traditional Protestant denominations. It involved churches pulling away from some of the ecumenical and social action commitments made during the 1960's. It provided data to help explain "why conservative churches are growing" (as opposed to liberal churches). It found sophisticated but forcefully clear expression by the eighteen Christian theologians who in January of 1975 drew up "The Hartford Appeal for Theological Affirmation"—a document that identified thirteen "pervasive, false, and debilitating themes in contemporary Christian thought."[21]

It would be false to conclude, however, that the majority of American Protestants simply are trying to return to some obscure or nostalgic past. Some, perhaps many, are moving in that direction. But there is no popular mass revival of "old-time religion." Church leaders seem to be searching for substantial theological affirmations to counteract the evaporating sense of American Protestant identity. Some are searching their traditions for essential faith commitments to mix with new theological currents. The growth or decline of traditional churches is not the only issue. More important is the reshaping of Christian traditions, and the developing of new ones, which might interact creatively with modern knowledge and oppressive social conditions. Even among conservative evangelical Protestants a new movement has begun away from easy identity with uncritical Americanism and toward a commitment to social criticism and reform. A significant moment in this developing evangelical identity occurred in 1973 when a conference of religious leaders meeting in Chicago signed the Declaration of Evangelical Social Concern. In January of 1976 a different ecumenical group of theologians produced The Boston Affirmations as a complement, if not an outright rebuttal, of the Hartford declaration of the previous year. Whereas in Hartford God's transcendence was recognized, in Boston God's involvement in humankind's historical struggle for justice and peace was celebrated.[22]

Only the combination of these two documents coming from two of the nation's oldest theological centers can suggest the depth and scope of the post-1960's quest of the American churches for Christian identity. It must not be forgotten, moreover, that there are many with Protestant rootage for whom traditional conceptions of God died, ethics became relative, and the churches turned irrelevant during the 1960's. They search theologically in new frontiers.

Protestant identity is at stake. Unless Protestantism is to become merely a catchall label for a conglomeration of conflicting or unrelated sects, plus a handful of largely bureaucratic but religiously nondescript denominations, it will have to engender a new sense of identity in its members. That identity will have to be broad and flexible enough to include liberal and conservative theological tendencies along with a large membership in between. But religious identity cannot be built simply on the least offensive or least controversial common theological denominator. Hence the Protestant dilemma is to find some kind of unity amid its theological extremes, without abandoning vital theological affirmation altogether. Moreover, religious identity is nourished by commitment and community experience. Unless Protestantism in its varieties can recover or develop some sense of corporate Christian identity, it will lose its creative force in the modern world.

It is not yet clear how damaging the demise of the Protestant empire in America has been to Protestant identity. Will American Protestantism be reborn in some new, nonimperial forms? Or is strictly Protestant identity bound to a historic epoch that has reached its climax, giving way to new Christian forms and alignments? It does not follow that a declining sense of Protestant identity inevitably fosters an accentuating Roman Catholic identity. Nor is the reverse true. The future seems more complex. Catholic identity also is at stake in America.

For Roman Catholics in America, the decade of the 1960's was even more explosive than it was for Protestants. Protestant identity had been crumbling for several decades, whereas this experience was new to many Catholics. The election of John F. Kennedy to the presidency, contrary to many Protestant fears and some Catholic hopes, resulted in no Roman Catholic take-over in America. More like the opposite happened. In every aspect of the church's life and thought major changes began to occur. The revival of high medieval scholastic theology, and the nearly unquestioned churchly obedience among the laity (and clergy), came to an abrupt end.

The Catholic leader in Rome as well as the one in the White House helped facilitate the church's burst into the modern world of the 1960's. Pope John XXIII deserted the triumphalist position and initiated the Second Vatican Council, whose statements on religious freedom and ecumenism changed American Catholicism to the point where the church of the 1950's seemed like ancient history. Meanwhile President Kennedy's programs and his broad appeal among all kinds of American people alleviated most Protestant fears that a Roman Catholic regime was about to introduce a foreign ecclesiastical oppression in American civil and religious life.

Internally, clergy and laity alike challenged the

church's authority and discipline. They introduced radical changes in the liturgy of worship. Their questioning of traditional morals and ethics ranged from not eating fish on Fridays to supporting birth control and abortion. They challenged traditional theology and dogmas, from the nature of the incarnation to papal infallibility. Such widely read European Catholic scholars as Hans Küng and Pierre Teilhard de Chardin furthered the new theological quest in America.

But that quest led to uncertainties as well as to reform and renewal. According to one perceptive Catholic interpreter of the situation, a deep "crisis of faith" set in, "symbolized by the reaction to the vernacular liturgy: 'now that we know what we believe we are not sure that we believe it.' "[23]

The external disruption of the church in American society was no less traumatic. Dramatic expressions of civil disobedience, most notably the Berrigans', weakened the traditional Catholic argument that Roman Catholicism fostered high respect for civil authority.

Now that the flames of the 1960's have died down, the embers reveal permanent changes in traditional Christianity in America. Like the Protestants, the Catholics are divided and publicly diverse: "The days of a Catholic bloc moving in lock step are gone for good in America."[24] Protestant and Catholic identities thus have broken down in one sense. But in another sense they have coalesced into a deeper quest for Christian identity beyond their traditional barriers. Indeed, Protestants and Roman Catholics entered the decade of the 1970's far more open to one another, far more knowledgeable about one another, than ever before in American history.

Some things are relatively certain about the future. Christians, along with adherents of other religions, must struggle with the nature of belief, of commitment to claims of truth, and with how religious commitments are translated into life in the modern world. In a society of many religions, of many truth claims, how does one find one's way?

The real issue at stake in the crises of Protestant and Catholic identity in modern America is the identity of Christianity itself. Perhaps even more far-reaching is the uncertainty about what it means to be a religious person, community, or nation as the twenty-first century approaches. It is increasingly common for Americans to describe themselves other than Protestant, Catholic, or Jew (or any other religion). At the same time people want to believe in something greater than themselves, their nation, or even all of nature. They are aware of some transcendent dimension of human existence, but they flounder without any sense of religious identity lodged and nourished in community experience. They lack a sense of identity with a dynamic tradition which might provide meaning to historic existence (past, present, future). Without the community, which Christianity calls the church, religious identity wanes for lack of shared reinforcement in discipline, commitment, mission, and celebration.

Americans are seeking meaning in life in a theological sense. But their questions are not posed exclusively in traditional thought forms. Nor are their questions answered exclusively by traditional

Christian dogmas. People are seeking within the
context of unprecedented knowledge about the
world and about life. They are seeking within the
context of seemingly uncontrollable forces of modern technological, military, and industrial power
which threaten life itself. They seek in the context
of the world religions in their midst.

Christians in modern America must struggle
with what it means to claim, believe, and live by
the faith that God was uniquely present in Jesus
Christ. Simply to make the claim, believe it, and
try to live by it is possible (though difficult). Many
will continue to follow this path. Conservative
churches will continue to grow. They are significant perpetuators of Christianity as a historic
world religion. They bring wholeness to life for
many faithful believers. They facilitate many car-
ing communities. They often make believers feel
safe from threatening forces of the world and
within themselves. Conservative churches, however, do not always do these things. Holding fast to
a particular theology does not guarantee Christian
community or even a living faith. But conservative
churches strongly endure partly because they provide a solid foundation of religious identity for
many Christians. They are valuable to society to
the degree that they contribute to forces of justice
and freedom for all people—those outside as well
as those within church memberships.

The modern world challenges Christians to look
beyond themselves. Christians sensitive to values
in other religions find it difficult to maintain their
distinctive religious identity. They take seriously
the historical fact that Christianity is one world

religion among several. Just as factual is the unique claim that Christianity makes about God's self-revelation in Jesus Christ. The question is: Can one affirm and live according to distinctively Christian insights and experiences while appreciating the distinctive insights and experiences of other religions? Can one be truly open to religious teachings other than one's own in such a way that one's faith and quality of life are increased? Can the meeting of different religions be mutually strengthening without destroying their distinctive values, creativity, and effectiveness in human life? Can the Christian gospel make sense, and be meaningfully communicated, within the modern world of knowledge and ideas?

Liberal-oriented Christians generally have concentrated on how to say "yes" to these kinds of questions. They have insisted that God's self-revelation in Jesus Christ indeed was unique, but not exclusive or exhausted. God also is known outside Christian circles. Therefore the Christian gospel must be understood and interpreted in the context of modern knowledge and experience which are broader than the Christian tradition. World religions must not simply coexist, but genuinely meet in dialogue and mutual learning.

It is true that the openness of liberal Christians to insights and experiences beyond Christianity frequently has not stimulated religious enthusiasm or zealous commitment. Their openness has not always contributed to a vital sense of Christian identity. But liberalism understands the gospel of Jesus Christ as itself being in the process of development beyond its first-century origins. History presents the unfolding of new meanings and implications of the divine revelation in Jesus Christ. Hence the Christian tradition is in fact developing. Christian identity cannot be pinned down to certain changeless structures, practices, or even doctrinal formulations. This means that liberal Christian identity is in flux. It always is threatened with extinction. It does not protect the faithful from the challenges of the world, but puts their religious identity on the line by engaging it in open dialogue with others. Many fall by the wayside—that is the risk. But it also is true that liberal churches, which do not always grow and which frequently die, have expressed at least as much sensitivity and service to human needs as have the more conservative churches. Service to humanity always has been a profound element in the Christian gospel, though not the most practiced.

Somehow the Christian spirit lives both in its more safe conservative forms and in its more risky liberal forms. A free and pluralistic society seems to require both forms of religious identity. One guards the religion's exclusiveness and particularity, which is necessary for its survival. The other brings the religion into creative dialogue with modern knowledge and other religions, which maintains its credibility as a faith applicable to all dimensions of human experience.

Infallible religious authorities, whether persons, institutions, literature, confessional statements, or spiritual experiences, finally do not prevail against all doubt or disbelief in the modern age. Somehow the "costly grace" of which Dietrich Bonhoeffer spoke in the 1930's cannot be identified with any

of these religious authorities. Yet it is extremely
unclear just what forms Christ's demands do take
in the complex modern world whether within or
outside these traditional religious authorities. Bonhoeffer was correct: "The issue can no longer be
evaded. It is becoming clearer every day that the
most urgent problem besetting our Church is this:
How can we live the Christian life in the modern
world?"[25]

Devout Christian seekers in our times may learn
from William James, who wrote in 1901: "He who
acknowledges the imperfections of his instrument,
and makes allowance for it in discussing his obser-
vations, is in a much better position for gaining
truth than if he claimed his instrument to be infallible." James recognized that "dogmatism will
doubtless continue to condemn us for this confession," but concluded nevertheless that "when
larger ranges of truth open, it is surely best to be
able to open ourselves to their reception, unfet-
tered by our previous pretensions."[26]

The previous pretensions of Christendom in
America must give way to larger ranges of truth
within the world of religions. The Christian belief
that the gospel of Jesus Christ speaks uniquely to
human needs cannot prevail in the form of cultural privilege. To follow Christ does not imply
receiving special secular favors. Nor does it mean
to withdraw from the world. Rather, it requires
serious involvement with the variety of religious
experiences and the multiple forms of oppressive
human conditions of our time.

Some historic Christian claims are vulnerable.
The claim, for example, that Christianity manifests

humankind's highest cultural and ethical achievement lacks historical persuasiveness. As a belief system and religious institution ingrained in powerful political and cultural forces, Christianity has been both creative and destructive. Frequently Christians have enjoyed their salvation at the expense of others. Today Christians must recognize that their religion has fallen short not only of Biblical demands and ideals but also of the highest visions of other religions. Christianity, no less than other religions, must be tested in our times.

If Christians are to embrace the First Amendment to the United States Constitution, and if they are to accept the coming of age of American religious pluralism, they must relinquish their pretense of Christendom. Christianity cannot dominate the world. Within the dialogue of pluralism, as in the spirit of some of the nation's founders, we might anticipate the visibility of higher values in human life if all religions are free to make their own way. Each must contribute to the common good. To the extent that Christians believe that truth will prevail, they have nothing to fear.

Meanwhile, concern with comparative religions of the world is no mere academic exercise. It is a living American experience. Many persons are religiously mobile, moving from religious groups and ideas to other religious groups and ideas. Broad ranges of religious experience in fact are open, which in a free society is something to celebrate. It can be a Christian celebration if understood as an extension of John Robinson's seventeenth-century Puritan acknowledgment that "the Lord hath more truth yet to break forth out of his Holy Word."[27]

For Christians to celebrate religious pluralism, however, is no simple matter. Pluralism implies essential differences among the traditions. These cannot be ignored or diminished without damaging the reality of pluralism and the integrity of its members. Just as the Euro-Americans, Afro-Americans, Hispanic-Americans, Asian-Americans, and Indian-Americans represent distinct cultural experiences, so are some of the essential religious experiences of Christians, Jews, Moslems, Buddhists, Hindus, and other traditions distinct. To preserve the fullness of human religious experience, each tradition must express its distinctive character freely—without special help or hindrance from civil authority. For this to happen is the beauty of a free and pluralistic society. But authentic pluralism requires Christians to struggle with the meaning and implications of their religious faith. The gospel of Jesus Christ makes particular claims about the divine reality in human history. The particularity of these claims can only be fully known when seriously related to the claims of other religions. Religious pluralism poses a threat to Christian commitment when Christians have not comprehended or experienced the essential value of their historic faith within the larger human experience.

My experience with the kind of ecumenical theological study taking place in Berkeley, California, has convinced me that students are able to understand and express the genius of their particular religious traditions best when directly confronted with students of other traditions. Dialogue and confrontation among differing religions can help develop new levels of human understanding and common concern without destroying the unique witness of each participant. Change may come to all traditions, but the essential and valuable distinctives persevere.

We should not conclude, therefore, that religious pluralism cancels out or invalidates theological commitments or religious values. Different religions are more or less intellectually stimulating, socially constructive, emotionally satisfying, aesthetically creative, and enduring for individuals and the larger social order. Americans will continue to distinguish among theological truth claims, and the various traditions will continue to provide arenas of religious identity. Christians have no choice but to affirm a unique experience of God incarnate in Jesus Christ. Their challenge will be to relate this affirmation to the world of many kinds of religious affirmations without losing their Christian integrity or ignoring the integrity of others.

Christians may draw upon the Biblical tradition for insights and experience of how life might be lived creatively in our times. Taking into account the many dimensions of suffering and tragedy, Christians might identify with forces of healing and justice. Christians might initiate some of these forces, and they might join forces initiated by others. This kind of Christian identity is drawn outward, not to triumph over but to serve humankind. The personal pilgrimage and the communal Christian experience can interact with other pilgrimages and communal experiences which make up the larger human condition. The ambiguities, contradictions, and defeats along the road of social betterment do not thereby excuse one from religious involvement in the struggle, just as they do not allow religious triumphalism. Therefore Christian identity and American nationhood might interact, but never again become identified.

The quest for humane values in the modern world may not be the ultimate Christian concern, but it should be a passion stimulated and nourished by commitment to the gospel of Jesus Christ. This passion should be one major identifying mark of the Christian in any culture. In the words of one modern Christian prophet, this passion is "the radical imperative."[28]

It seems to me that the critical arena of dialogue in America's third century will be not only among the various religions but even more between the religious and secular dimensions of human life. What does it mean to be religious in a secular age? Together the religious traditions must help inspire human beings to project humane goals, and humane means to achieving those goals. At stake is human survival in the earth's limited space and resources. Secular technology, which has helped create the crisis of life, now must be utilized to help solve the problems. The religious and the secular therefore must work together. Religions that are worldwide in scope have the potential to infuse ethical values into worldwide secular technocracy. But those religions which transcend nations and cultures must come to recognize their potential power as ethical forces in the world. It is by no means clear that this is possible. Nevertheless, the challenge, though unprecedented in scope and consequence, looms before us. Surely one cannot be Christian and American with any credibility without confronting this worldwide challenge.

Can the Christian faith claim to be universally valid while recognizing the validity of other religious faiths? Of course! Just as other religions can make this claim and be universal in fact, which means to be inclusive of all kinds of persons in all kinds of places. Alongside other religions, Christianity can be represented among all peoples and can seek the well-being of all peoples without feeling pressed to make all peoples and all cultures Christian. Christians can in fact know God uniquely through Jesus Christ while rejoicing that others know God differently through other historic channels. Christians, who experience their salvation in Jesus Christ, can live their faith freely without apology, yet respect the freedom of others to follow different spiritual roads.

Similar things can be said about the American nation. As Christians must discover their integrity alongside and in mutual respect for the integrity of other religions, so must America discover its national integrity alongside and in mutual respect for other nations. As truth is within, but also outside the Christian religion, so universally valid ideals and values of human society are within but also beyond the American nation. The implications of this line of thought may be revolutionary to some, idealistic to others, and heretical to still others. But what is a realistic alternative?

Therefore we have arrived at the notion of Christian identity *in* but not *of* the nation: Christianity transcending America in the churches' global life, and America transcending Christianity in the nation's pluralistic life. For America does not exist by Christians alone; and Christians do not live by the grace of America.

Appendix:
Church—Sect—Denomination

Scholars long have debated over how best to categorize the variety of American Christian modes of self-understanding and patterns of organization. Some have tried to apply the European understanding of "church type" and "sect type" to American conditions. Most influential has been H. Richard Niebuhr's classic study *The Social Sources of Denominationalism* (1929). He defined the *church* as "a natural social group akin to the family or the nation." Membership in a church is popular, even "socially obligatory"; for the church is "closely allied with national, economic, and cultural interests." In contrast, the *sect* is a "voluntary association" of persons held together by some particular type of belief or religious experience. Sects are religious minority groups consciously separated from the "worldly" religion of the majority church. Furthermore, "members are born into the church while they must join the sect."

> Churches are inclusive institutions, frequently are national in scope, and emphasize the universalism of the gospel; while sects are exclusive in charac-

ter, appeal to the individualistic element in Christianity, and emphasize its ethical demands.[1]

These categories never have applied as well to America as to European Christianity, because in America there is no state church and all Christian groups are essentially voluntary associations. Scholars have found, therefore, that the word "denomination" better describes the various kinds of Christian groups in America. But whereas denominationalism as a principle, theory, or type of organization has been defined rather clearly, it has not been found operating precisely or consistently in American Christianity.[2]

My definition of a denomination is as follows: *an organization of religious groups (such as congregations) representing a tradition of doctrine, discipline, worship, structure, and order, and in some cases also racial, ethnic, or nationality groupings.* A denomination is neither a sect nor a church as these generally have been understood. Yet it contains both sectarian and churchly tendencies, and it can lean heavily in either direction.

Insofar as denominations acknowledge one another as valid and full expressions of Christianity, existing together on an equal basis in the nation, they reflect a churchly Christian identity. But to the extent that they express their autonomy, emphasize their distinctive characteristics, and maintain special requirements for membership, they assume a more sectarian Christian identity.

Denominational Christianity has expressed itself in some strange and confusing ways in America. Roman Catholicism, for example, the most direct descendant of Christendom's church, had to take on some characteristics of a nonconforming sectarian role in the nineteenth century. Yet it never gave up its churchly aspirations. At the same time Baptists, who originated as a separatist Puritan sect, developed some churchly forms as the dominant organized religious force in the American South. Yet they never relinquished many of their sectarian attitudes. Both Roman Catholics and Southern Baptists, the two largest Christian denominations in America, in sectarian fashion held fast to their own exclusive claims to truth and disassociated themselves from other Christian denominations.

To some extent every denomination senses its own superior expression of Christianity. This kind of sectarian conviction is partly what holds the group together and keeps it going. Yet many persons relate to a denomination primarily out of convenience or habit. They might just as well join another denominational church were it to become more practical to do so. After all, they reason, are not all churches teaching basically the same thing? Out of this understanding, especially among Protestants, many American Christians have been religiously mobile, moving from church to church regardless of denominational affiliation.

Some Christian distinctions have been more rigid. On the whole the so-called nineteenth-century "mainline" Protestant traditions assumed the denominational label exclusively for themselves. As the popular and socially "respectable" Christians, they became America's nineteenth-century *churches.* Other groups were described as the

small *sects,* or in the case of Roman Catholicism as
a minority *church.* Partly because of the Protestant identification with denominationalism, until
recent years Roman Catholics rejected the label
for themselves. Christian identity surely has borne
the confusion of traditional labels not quite adapt-
able to the American situation.

I am suggesting in this book that *church* and *sect*
do correlate, though imprecisely, with the two basic kinds of religious orientation within which
Christians have asserted their sense of identity in
America. Chapters 1, 2, and 3 focus largely on
sectarian tendencies; while Chapter 4 describes
the more churchly tendencies. Chapter 5 points to
the present-day disappearance of mainline Christianity (churches) as over against minority Christian
groups (sects) in America. All religious groups are
minorities, all are becoming denominations in fact
as well as in theory. They present an almost unlimited variation of churchly and sectarian mixtures
in the quest for Christian identity in America.

Notes

INTRODUCTION

1. In this book, "religious pluralism" is defined simply as follows: different, separate, autonomous religious organizations and traditions, each with its own particular identity and constituency, yet all existing alongside one another within the same society.

2. See the Appendix for a brief technical discussion of the developing categories of church, sect, and denomination.

Chapter 1. THE AMERICAN RELIGIOUS REVOLUTION

1. Sydney E. Ahlstrom, *A Religious History of the American People* (Yale University Press, 1972), p. 4.

2. Isaac Backus, *Government and Liberty Described and Ecclesiastical Tyranny Exposed* (1778), printed in Robert L. Ferm (ed.), *Issues in American Protestantism: A Documentary History from the Puritans to the Present* (Doubleday & Company, Inc., 1969), p. 109.

3. James Madison, "Memorial and Remonstrance" (1786), portions printed in Edwin Scott Gaustad (ed.), *Religious Issues in American History* (Harper & Row, Publishers, Inc., 1968), p. 72.

4. Tensions between religious convictions and civic responsibilities, and between religious freedom and civil laws, demonstrate historically that the implications and limitations of the First Amendment are complex. For the purpose of this book, particularly Chapter 5, my understanding of the problem has been instructed especially by two recent articles: David Little, "The Origins of Perplexity: Civil Religion and Moral Belief in the Thought of Thomas Jefferson," in Russell E. Richey and Donald G. Jones (eds.), *American Civil Religion* (Harper & Row, Publishers, Inc., 1974), pp. 185–210; and Leo Pfeffer, "The Legitimation of Marginal Religions in the United States," and John Richard Burkholder, "The Law Knows No Heresy: Marginal Religious Movements and the Courts," in Irving I. Zaretsky and Mark P. Leone (eds.), *Religious Movements in Contemporary America* (Princeton University Press, 1974), pp. 9–50.

5. Immigration statistics are taken from Ahlstrom, *A Religious History of the American People*, pp. 749–750.

6. Frederick C. Luebke, *Bonds of Loyalty: German-Americans and World War I* (Northern Illinois University Press, 1974), pp. 34–35.

7. For a Unitarian-transcendentalist version, see, for example, Theodore Parker's 1841 sermon, "The Transient and Permanent in Christianity," printed in Conrad Wright (ed.), *Three Prophets of Religious Liberalism: Channing—Emerson—Parker* (Beacon Press, Inc., 1961). The Disciples of Christ position was expressed by Thomas Campbell, one of the movement's early voices, in his 1809 "Declaration and Address," printed in H. Shelton Smith, Robert T. Handy, and Lefferts A. Loetscher (eds.), *American Christianity: An Historical Interpretation with Representative Documents* (Charles Scribner's Sons, 1963), Vol. I, pp. 578–586. The Roman Catholic debate can be seen in John

Ireland, "The Church and the Age," in *The Church and Modern Society* (St. Paul, Minn.: The Pioneer Press, 1905), Vol. I, pp. 112–115, countered by Thomas Preston, "American Catholicity," *American Catholic Quarterly Review,* Vol. XVI (1891), pp. 399 ff.

8. Charles G. Finney, *Lectures on Revivals of Religion* (Leavitt, Lord and Co., 1835; reprint, Harvard University Press, Belknap Press, 1960), pp. 269–270.

9. From John W. Nevin, *The Anxious Bench* (Second Edition, Revised and Enlarged, 1844), portions reprinted in Ferm (ed.), *Issues in American Protestantism,* pp. 170–180.

10. The most widely accepted definition is found in the *Scofield Reference Bible* (first published in 1909), note 4 following Gen. 1:27: "A dispensation is a period of time during which man is tested in respect of obedience to some *specific* revelation of the will of God."

11. Winthrop S. Hudson, *Religion in America,* 2d ed. (Charles Scribner's Sons, 1973), p. 350.

12. Quoted in Frederick E. Mayer, *Religious Bodies of America* (Concordia Publishing House, 1956), pp. 316–317.

13. Frances Trollope, *The Domestic Manners of the Americans* (1832), excerpts printed in Milton Powell (ed.), *The Voluntary Church: American Religious Life (1740–1865) Seen Through the Eyes of European Visitors* (The Macmillan Company, 1967), pp. 67–73.

14. Philip Schaff, *America: A Sketch of Its Political, Social, and Religious Character,* ed. by Perry Miller (Harvard University Press, 1961), p. 80.

Chapter 2. CHRISTIANS ESTRANGED

1. For a discussion of the difference between "church" and "sect," see the Appendix.

2. Rufus M. Jones, *The Faith and Practice of the Quakers* (London: Methuen & Co., 1927), p. 123.

3. See Fred W. Evans, *Compendium of the Origins, Principles, Rules and Regulations, Government, and Doctrines of the United Society of Believers in Christ's Second Appearing* (D. Appleton and Co., 1859).

4. R. L. Williams, "Shakers, Now Only 12, Observe Their 200th Year," *Smithsonian,* Vol. V (Summer, 1974), pp. 40–49.

5. Trusteeism is further discussed in Chapter 4.

6. Father Alexander Czitkovicz, C.SS.R., to the Society for the Propagation of the Faith (1844), published in John Tracy Ellis, (ed.), *Documents of American Catholic History* (The Bruce Publishing Company, 1962), p. 268.

7. Quotations from John A. Hostetler, *Mennonite Life* (Herald Press, 1954), p. 36; and *Amish Life* (Herald Press, 1952), pp. 6–8.

8. Joseph F. Zygmut, "Prophetic Failure and Chiliastic Identity: The Case of Jehovah's Witnesses," *American Journal of Sociology,* Vol. LXXV, No. 6 (May, 1970), pp. 926–948.

9. J. Howard Pew, "Should the Church 'Meddle' in Civil Affairs?" *Reader's Digest,* May, 1966, pp. 49–54.

10. As the definition of religion has broadened in recent years, scholars (especially sociologists) have found it increasingly difficult to pin down the meaning of secularity. Recognizing this difficulty, I nevertheless can find no better term by which to designate the areas of modern life commonly thought to be void of religion or outside the realm of religion. Specifically, I relate secularization to the historical breakup of Christendom wherein during the past four hundred years or so Christianity and the church have permeated less and less of social, political, economic, and intellectual life in the Western world. I find expecially helpful the definition of secularization set forth by Peter L. Berger, *The Sacred Canopy: Elements of a Sociological Theory of Religion* (Doubleday & Company, Inc., 1969), p. 107; and

the essays in James F. Childress and David B. Harned (eds.), *Secularization and the Protestant Prospect* (The Westminster Press, 1970).

11. By "subculture" I do not mean to imply a lower quality or form of culture or one of secondary importance. Rather, I mean simply a minority culture with respect to the dominant cultural forces of the nation.

12. The Book of Mormon, 1 Nephi 13:1–19; 2 Nephi 10:11–12.

13. Bruce Kinney, *Mormonism the Islam of America* (Fleming H. Revell Company, 1912), is one example.

14. Thomas F. O'Dea, "Sources of Strain in Mormon History Reconsidered," in Marvin S. Hill and James B. Allen (eds.), *Mormonism and American Culture* (Harper & Row, Publishers, Inc., 1972), p. 150.

15. Quoted by Richard L. Evans, "What Is a Mormon?" in Leo Rosten (ed.), *Religions of America: Ferment and Faith in an Age of Crisis* (Simon & Schuster, Inc., 1975), p. 195.

16. Douglass' speech is printed in Herbert Aptheker (ed.), *A Documentary History of the Negro People in the United States* (The Citadel Press, 1969), pp. 331–334.

17. Quoted in Larry George Murphy, "The Church and Black Californians: A Mid-Nineteenth-Century Struggle for Civil Justice," *Foundations*, Vol. XVIII, No. 2 (April–June, 1975), p. 176.

18. C. Eric Lincoln, *The Black Church Since Frazier* (Schocken Books, Inc., 1974), pp. 107–108. The previous quotations are from Eugene D. Genovese, *Roll, Jordan, Roll: The World the Slaves Made* (Pantheon Books, Inc., 1974), p. 281; and W. E. B. Du Bois, *The Souls of Black Folk: Essays and Sketches* (Fawcett Publications, 1961 edition), p. 16.

19. Henry H. Mitchell, *Black Belief: Folk Beliefs of Blacks in America and West Africa* (Harper & Row, Publishers, Inc., 1975), pp. 9, 11.

Chapter 3. CHRISTIAN DISSENT

1. Edwin Scott Gaustad, *Dissent in American Religion* (The University of Chicago Press, 1973), p. 3. See also Jeffrey B. Russell (ed.), *Religious Dissent in the Middle Ages* (John Wiley & Sons, Inc., 1971).

2. James H. Cone, *Black Theology and Black Power* (The Seabury Press, Inc., 1969), p. 92; and Major J. Jones, *Black Awareness: A Theology of Hope* (Abingdon Press, 1971), p. 46.

3. The words of Rev. T. M. Ward, printed in *Appeal*, July 26, 1862, p. 2.

4. Murphy, "The Church and Black Californians," pp. 180–181.

5. For Booker T. Washington's outlook, see especially his *The Future of the American Negro* (Boston: Small, Maynard & Co., 1902); and his autobiography, *Up from Slavery* (Doubleday, Page, & Co., 1901).

6. The statement is printed in Nathan Wright, Jr., *Black Power* (Hawthorn Books, Inc., 1967), pp. 187–194.

7. The letter is printed in Conrad Cherry (ed.), *God's New Israel: Religious Interpretations of American Destiny* (Prentice-Hall, Inc., 1971), pp. 347–360.

8. Murphy, "The Church and Black Californians," p. 178.

9. Quoted in Page Smith, *Daughters of the Promised Land: Women in American History* (Little, Brown & Company, 1970), p. 143.

10. Theressa Hoover, "Black Women and the Church: Triple Jeopardy," in Alice L. Hageman (ed.), *Sexist Religion and Women in the Church: No More Silence!* (Association Press, 1974), pp. 64–66.

11. Joan Arnold Romero, "The Protestant Principle: A Woman's-Eye View of Barth and Tillich," in Rosemary Radford Ruether (ed.), *Religion and Sexism: Images of Woman in the Jewish and Christian Traditions* (Simon & Schuster, Inc., 1974), p. 319.

12. Julia Cherry Spruill, *Women's Life and Work in the Southern Colonies* (W. W. Norton & Company, Inc., 1972 edition), p. 254; and Janet Wilson James, "Introduction" to *Notable American Women 1607–1950,* 3 vols. (Harvard University Press, Belknap Press, 1971), Vol. I, p. xxvi.

13. Quoted from writings of the Grimke sisters printed in Alice S. Rossi (ed.), *The Feminist Papers: From Adams to de Beauvoir* (Bantam Books, 1974), pp. 304, 307.

14. Quoted by Matilda Joslyn Gage, "Women, Church, and State," in Elizabeth Cady Stanton, Susan B. Anthony, and Matilda Joslyn Gage (eds.), *History of Woman Suffrage* (Rochester, N.Y.: Fowler and Wells, 1887), Vol. I, pp. 784, 791.

15. Quoted by Anna A. Gordon, *The Beautiful Life of Frances E. Willard* (Evanston, Ill.: Women's Temperance Publishing Association, 1898), p. 114.

16. Preface to *The Woman's Bible* (New York: European Publishing Company, 1895), Part I, p. 12.

17. *Ibid.,* p. 74. *The Woman's Bible* first was brought to my attention by Suzan E. Hill, who subsequently wrote "The Woman's Bible: The Religious Impulse of Nineteenth-Century Feminism and Its Struggle with Christianity" (unpublished M.A. thesis, San Francisco Theological Seminary, 1976).

18. Sheila D. Collins, "Toward a Feminist Theology," *The Christian Century,* Aug. 2, 1972.

19. Henry Zwaanstra, *Reformed Thought and Experience in a New World: A Study of the Christian Reformed Church and Its American Environment 1890–1918* (Kampen, Netherlands: J. H. Kok, 1973), p. 138.

Chapter 4. AMERICAN CHRISTENDOM

1. John Adams, "Thoughts on Government," January, 1776, printed in Adrienne Koch (ed.), *The American Enlightenment: The Shaping of the American Ex-*

periment and a Free Society (G. Braziller, 1965), p. 250.

2. From "The Young American," *Dial,* Vol. IV (April, 1844), pp. 484–507.

3. From John Ireland, "Human Progress," in *The Church and Modern Society,* Vol. I, pp. 157–158.

4. Isaac M. Wise, "Our Country's Place in History" (1869), printed in Cherry (ed.), *God's New Israel,* p. 227.

5. Quoted in Yehoshua Arieli, *Individualism and Nationalism in American Ideology* (Penguin Books, 1966), p. 268.

6. See Ch. V of Sidney E. Mead, *The Lively Experiment: The Shaping of Christianity in America* (Harper & Row, Publishers, Inc., 1963), pp. 72 ff.

7. See Perry Miller, *Errand Into the Wilderness* (Harvard University Press, Belknap Press, 1956).

8. Jonathan Edwards and Ezra Stiles are quoted in Cherry (ed.), *God's New Israel,* pp. 55–59, 82–89.

9. Quoted in Glenn T. Miller, "The American Revolution as a Religious Event," *Foundations,* Vol. XIX, No. 2 (April–June, 1976). Brockway made the common error of discounting the American Indians as inhabitants of the American frontier.

10. On the denominational principles, see the Appendix.

11. Robert Baird, *Religion in America* (Harper & Brothers, 1844), p. 220.

12. Schaff, *America: A Sketch of Its Political, Social, and Religious Character,* p. 76.

13. *Home Mission Record,* Dec., 1849, p. 13; March, 1854, p. 22; April, 1858, p. 12; and American Baptist Home Mission Society *Annual Report,* 1851, pp. 68–71; 1855, p. 57.

14. Harriet Beecher Stowe, "Appeal to the Women of America," from Charles Edward Stowe, *The Life of Harriet Beecher Stowe* (Houghton Mifflin and Company, 1891), pp. 255–261.

15. Samuel S. Hill, Jr., *et al., Religion and the Solid*

South (Abingdon Press, 1972), p. 25.

16. The words of the "Battle Hymn of the Republic" were written by Julia Ward Howe in 1861.

17. Phillips Brooks, "Need of an Enthusiasm for Humanity on the Part of the Churches," *National Needs and Remedies,* (New York: Baker and Taylor, 1890), p. 301.

18. Quoted in Timothy L. Smith, *Revivalism and Social Reform: American Protestantism on the Eve of the Civil War* (Abingdon Press, 1957), pp. 221–222.

19. J. G. Butler, "Is Our Nation Christian?—A Centennial Thought," *The Quarterly Review of the Evangelical Lutheran Church,* Vol. VI, No. 4 (Oct., 1876), pp. 510–525.

20. Howard B. Grose, *Aliens or Americans?* (New York: Young People's Missionary Movement, 1906), p. 255.

21. Rauschenbusch's entire sermon was published in the Rochester *Post Express,* Nov. 25, 1898.

22. Josiah Strong, *Our Country: Its Possible Future and Its Present Crisis,* ed. by Jurgen Herbst (Harvard University Press, 1963), p. 13; and *Expansion Under New World Conditions* (New York, 1900), p. 302.

23. John R. Mott, *The Present World Situation* (New York: Student Volunteer Movement for Foreign Missions, 1914), p. 122.

24. Ernest De Witt Burton, "The Challenge of the Present Crisis," *The New World Movement* (American Baptist Board of Education, 1919), p. 10.

25. E. M. Wood, *Methodism and the Centennial of American Independence* (New York: Nelson and Phillips, 1876), pp. 295–296.

26. D. C. Eddy, *Immigration* (New York: The Judson Printing Company, 1889), pp. 2, 6.

27. Samuel Eliot Morison, *The European Discovery of America,* Vol. 2: *The Southern Voyages, A.D. 1492–1616* (Oxford University Press, 1974), pp. 52–53.

28. From Carroll's 1773 correspondence, quoted in Ellis (ed.), *Documents of American Catholic History* (The Bruce Publishing Company, 1962), p. 129.

29. Quoted in John Tracy Ellis, *American Catholicism* (The University of Chicago Press, 1956), p. 70.

30. Quoted in Ellis (ed.), *Documents of American Catholic History*, p. 231; and Sebastian G. Messmer (ed.), *The Works of the Right Reverend John England, First Bishop of Charleston* (Cleveland, Ohio: Arthur H. Clark Co., 1908), Vol. VII, p. 73.

31. Quoted in Lawrence Kehoe, *The Complete Works of the Most Rev. John Hughes* (New York: The American News Co., 1864), Vol. I, Part V, p. 9.

32. Quoted in Ellis (ed.), *Documents of American Catholic History*, p. 341.

33. Quoted in James F. Cleary, "Catholic Participation in the World's Parliament of Religions, Chicago, 1893," *The Catholic Historical Review*, Vol. LV (Jan., 1970), p. 603.

34. These quotations from AFCS conventions are found in *Proceedings of the Second National Convention of the American Federation of Catholic Societies* (Chicago, Aug. 5–7, 1902), p. 8; and *Bulletin of the American Federation of Catholic Societies*, Vol. V (Nov.–Dec., 1911), p. 3, and Vol. VII (Dec., 1913), p. 2. I am indebted to Alfred J. Ede for directing me to these sources, especially in his unpublished Graduate Theological Union seminar paper, "The Catholic Crusade for a Christian America: A Study of the American Federation of Catholic Societies 1900–1917."

35. *Monitor* (San Francisco Archdiocese), May 15, 1909.

36. *New Era Magazine*, Vol. I (Sept., 1919), p. 522.

37. *Brownson's Quarterly Review*, Vol. XXII (April, 1860), pp. 253–261. For the "stamp of Geneva," see Winthrop S. Hudson, *American Protestantism* (The University of Chicago Press, 1961), p. 18.

38. *Home Mission Record,* Jan., 1854, p. 13; and J. E. Benton, *California—As She Was; As She Is; As She Is to Be* (Placer Times Press, 1850).

Chapter 5. CHRISTIANITY IN BUT NOT OF THE NATION

1. On secularization, see Chapter 2, note 10.
2. See Walter Laidlaw (ed.), *The Moral Aims of the War* (Fleming H. Revell Company, 1918).
3. *The Baptist,* Sept. 25, 1920, p. 1199.
4. Halford E. Luccock, *Contemporary American Literature and Religion* (Willett, Clark & Company, 1934), p. 43.
5. Such books as Henry Churchill King, *Seeing Life Whole* (1923); Charles Reynolds Brown, *Why I Believe in Religion* (1924); J. Arthur Thomson, *Science and Religion* (1925); Charles E. deM. Sajous, *Strength of Religion as Shown by Science* (1926); Ernest De Witt Burton, *Christianity in the Modern World* (1927); Horace M. Kallen, *Why Religion* (1927); and Paul Arthur Schilpp, *Do We Need Religion?* (1929).
6. Walter Marshall Horton, *Contemporary Continental Theology* (Harper & Brothers, 1938), p. 84. Previous quotations are from *The Modern Schoolman,* Vol. I (Jan., 1925), p. 8, and (Feb., 1925), pp. 7–8. The most thorough study of post-World War I Thomistic revival in America is William A. Halsey's "The Survival of American Innocence: Catholic Thought in an Era of Disillusionment 1920–1945" (unpublished Ph.D. dissertation, Graduate Theological Union, 1976).
7. For example, "Growing Protestant Concern Over the Number of Catholics," *Newsweek,* Vol. XXVIII (Sept. 2, 1946), p. 68; "Fear of Catholic Proselytizing," *The Christian Century,* Vol. LXVII (March 15, 1950), p. 323; "Catholic Census," *Newsweek,* Vol. XXXV (June 12, 1950), p. 78; "Those Church Statistics,"

Time, Vol. LXVI (Oct. 31, 1955), p. 37; and "If the United States Becomes 51% Catholic," *Christianity Today,* Vol. VII (Oct. 27, 1958), pp. 8–12. For comparative Protestant-Catholic statistics, see André Siegfried, *America at Mid-Century,* tr. by Margaret Ledésert (Harcourt, Brace & Company, 1955), p. 87. These sources and those in notes 8 to 10 following were brought to my attention by Carol Hyland, "Inter-Faith Dynamics Through Censorship, 1948–1957" (unpublished M.A. thesis, Graduate Theological Union, 1974).

8. For example, "Catholics Invade Rural America," *The Christian Century,* Vol. LXII (Jan. 10, 1945), p. 44; "Catholics Find It Pays to Advertise," *Newsweek,* Vol. XXXIV (Aug. 29, 1949), p. 64; "The Roman Catholic Church and Censorship," *The Converted Catholic,* Vol. XIII (Sept., 1952), p. 216; James H. Nichols, "What Disturbs Protestants About Catholics," *Look* (May 18, 1954), p. 47; and "Sense or Censor," *Pulpit,* Vol. XXVIII (March, 1957), p. 7.

9. For example, "How Catholic Congressmen Voted," *Information Service,* Vol. XXVIII (April 2, 1949), p. 3; "Is There Really a Catholic Vote?" *U.S. News & World Report,* Vol. XLI (Aug. 17, 1956), p. 42; and "Can the Catholic Vote Swing the Election?" *U.S. News & World Report,* Vol. XLI (Oct. 10, 1956), p. 41.

10. For example, Conrad Henry Moehlman, *The Catholic-Protestant Mind* (New York, 1929); and Charles Clayton Morrison, *Can Protestantism Win America?* (Harper & Brothers, 1948); "Can Catholicism Win America?" *The Christian Century,* Vol. LXI (Nov. 29, 1944), p. 1378; "Is Protestantism Slipping?" *Time,* Vol. LII (Feb. 23, 1948), p. 72; "Protestant Concern Over Catholics," *American Mercury,* Vol. LXV (Sept. 1949), p. 264; "Can Protestantism Survive?" *Advance,* Vol. CXLIX (Sept. 1, 1957), p. 5; and "A Catholic United States?" *Time,* Vol. LXVI (Jan. 22, 1955), p. 64.

11. *The New York Times,* June 12, 1947, p. 1.

12. For the variety of Catholic social movements during these years, see David J. O'Brien, *American Catholics and Social Reform: The New Deal Years* (Oxford University Press, 1968).

13. Two of the more influential studies along this line were Will Herberg, *Protestant—Catholic—Jew: An Essay in American Religious Sociology* (Doubleday & Company, Inc., 1955), and E. Digby Baltzell, *The Protestant Establishment: Aristocracy and Caste in America* (Random House, Inc., 1964).

14. Robert T. Handy, *A Christian America: Protestant Hopes and Historical Realities* (Oxford University Press, 1971), Ch. VII.

15. *The Berkeley Daily Gazette*, Nov. 1, 1975, pp. 1–2.

16. *San Francisco Chronicle*, Dec. 9, 1975, p. 1.

17. Carol Tewksbury, "Confession of a Dilettante," *San Francisco Chronicle*, Dec. 1, 1974. Letters to the editor appeared on Dec. 12, 1974.

18. These quotations from Supreme Court decisions are printed in Anson Phelps Stokes, *Church and State in the United States*, revised one-volume edition by Stokes and Leo Pfeffer (Harper & Row, Publishers, Inc., 1964), p. 563.

19. Michael Novak, "Christianity: Renewed or Slowly Abandoned?" in William G. McLoughlin and Robert N. Bellah (eds.), *Religion in America* (Beacon Press, Inc., 1968), p. 401.

20. Duncan Howlett, *The Fourth American Faith* (Beacon Press, Inc., 1964).

21. Peter L. Berger and Richard John Neuhaus (eds.), *Against the World for the World: The Hartford Appeal and the Future of American Religion* (The Seabury Press, Inc., 1976). On conservative churches, see Dean M. Kelley, *Why Conservative Churches Are Growing* (Harper & Row, Publishers, Inc., 1972). On the evangelical impulse, see Donald G. Bloesch, *The Evangelical Renaissance* (Wm. B. Eerdmans Publishing Company,

1973), and David F. Wells and John D. Woodbridge (eds.), *The Evangelicals: What They Believe, Who They Are, Where They Are Changing* (Abingdon Press, 1975), pp. 9–16.

22. On the Boston Affirmations, see the several articles in *Andover Newton Quarterly*, Vol. XVI (March, 1976). On the Declaration of Evangelical Social Concern, see Richard Quebedeaux, *The Young Evangelicals: Revolution in Orthodoxy* (Harper and Row, Publishers, Inc., 1974).

23. Dorothy Dohen, "The New Quest of American Catholicism," in Elwyn A. Smith (ed.), *The Religion of the Republic* (Fortress Press, 1971), pp. 79–80.

24. George Devine, *American Catholicism: Where Do We Go from Here?* (Prentice-Hall, Inc., 1975), p. 116.

25. Dietrich Bonhoeffer, *The Cost of Discipleship*, rev. ed., tr. by Reginald H. Fuller (The Macmillan Company, 1959), p. 47.

26. William James, *The Varieties of Religious Experience* (The New American Library of World Literature, Inc., Mentor Books, 1958), p. 260.

27. Quoted from John Robinson's famous speech on the occasion of the departure of some of the exiled Puritan Congregationalists in Leyden for Virginia, in Horton Davies, *The English Free Churches* (London: Oxford University Press, 1952), p. 56.

28. John C. Bennett, *The Radical Imperative: From Theology to Social Ethics* (The Westminster Press, 1975).

APPENDIX

1. H. Richard Niebuhr, *The Social Sources of Denominationalism* (The World Publishing Company, 1957 edition), pp. 17–19.

2. In my judgment the most convincing definitions

of the denominational principle in American Christianity are found in Hudson, *American Protestantism*, pp. 33–48; and Mead, *The Lively Experiment: The Shaping of Christianity in America*, pp. 103–104. An excellent discussion of the interpretation of various types of religious organizations in American historiography is John F. Wilson, "The Historical Study of Marginal American Religious Movements," in Zaretsky and Leone (eds.), *Religious Movements in Contemporary America*, pp. 596–611.

Suggested Reading

The most valuable bibliographical guide in the study of American religious history is Nelson R. Burr's two-volume *A Critical Bibliography of Religion in America* (Princeton University Press, 1961). Four survey histories of religion in America have appeared in the 1960's and 1970's: Clifton E. Olmstead, *History of Religion in the United States* (Prentice-Hall, Inc., 1960); Edwin Scott Gaustad, *A Religious History of America* (Harper & Row, Publishers, Inc., 1966); Winthrop S. Hudson, *Religion in America*, 2d ed. (Charles Scribner's Sons, 1973); and most recently the comprehensive work by Sydney E. Ahlstrom, *A Religious History of the American People* (Yale University Press, 1972), which includes an extensive bibliography.

Concerned exclusively with Christianity is the two-volume work by H. Shelton Smith, Robert T. Handy, and Lefferts A. Loetscher (eds.), *American Christianity: An Historical Interpretation with Representative Documents* (Charles Scribner's Sons, 1960–1963). Interpretative essays dealing mainly with Christianity are Sidney E. Mead, *The Lively Experiment: The Shaping of Christianity in America* (Harper & Row, Publishers, Inc., 1963), and William A. Clebsch, *From Sacred to Profane America: The Role of Religion in American History* (Harper & Row, Publishers, Inc., 1968).

Recent interpretations of American Protestant history are as follows: Winthrop S. Hudson, *American Protestantism* (The University of Chicago Press, 1961); Martin E. Marty, *Righteous Empire: The Protestant Experience in America* (The Dial Press, Inc., 1970); and Robert T. Handy, *A Christian America: Protestant Hopes and Historical Realities* (Oxford University Press, 1971). Concerned specifically with what I have called "post-Christendom" is Franklin H. Littell, *The Church and the Body Politic* (The Seabury Press, Inc., 1969). Two books focus on the evangelical tradition: William G. McLoughlin (ed.), *The American Evangelicals, 1800–1900* (Harper & Row, Publishers, Inc., 1968), and David F. Wells and John D. Woodbridge (eds.), *The Evangelicals: What They Believe, Who They Are, Where They Are Changing* (Abingdon Press, 1975). The standard reference work on the Mennonite-Amish movement is the four-volume work by Harold S. Bender and C. Henry Smith (eds.), *The Mennonite Encyclopedia* (Herald Press, 1959). Studies of theology include the following: Kenneth Cauthen, *The Impact of American Religious Liberalism* (Harper & Row, Publishers, Inc., 1962); Sydney E. Ahlstrom (ed.), *Theology in America: The Major Protestant Voices from Puritanism to Neo-Orthodoxy* (Yale University Press, 1967); William R. Hutchison (ed.), *American Protestant Thought: The Liberal Era* (Harper & Row, Publishers, Inc., 1968); Langdon Gilkey, "Social and Intellectual Sources of Contemporary Protestant Theology in America," in William G. McLoughlin and Robert N. Bellah (eds.), *Religion in America* (Beacon Press Inc., 1968); and William A. Clebsch, *American Religious Thought: A History* (The University of Chicago Press, 1973). A useful source is Robert L. Ferm (ed.), *Issues in American Protestantism: A Documentary History from the Puritans to the Present* (Doubleday & Company, Inc., 1969).

Recent interpretations of American Catholic history are as follows: Andrew M. Greeley, *The Catholic Experience: An Interpretation of the History of American Catholicism* (Doubleday & Company, Inc., 1967); John Tracy Ellis, *American Catholicism*, 2d rev. ed. (The University of Chicago Press, 1969); Philip Gleason (ed.), *Catholicism in America* (Harper & Row, Publishers, Inc., 1970); David J. O'Brien, *The Renewal of American Catholicism* (Oxford University Press, 1972); and George Devine, *American Catholicism: Where Do We Go from Here?* (Prentice-Hall, Inc., 1975). Of great value are two volumes containing source material: John Tracy Ellis (ed.), *Documents of American Catholic History*, 2d ed. (Bruce Publishing Company, 1962), and Aaron I. Abell (ed.), *American Catholic Thought on Social Questions* (The Bobbs-Merrill Company, Inc., 1968).

Among the many studies being published on the black churches in American history are E. Franklin Frazier, *The Negro Church in America*, and C. Eric Lincoln, *The Black Church Since Frazier* (Schocken Books, Inc., 1974); Joseph R. Washington, Jr., *Black Religion: The Negro and Christianity in the United States* (Beacon Press, Inc., 1964); Carter G. Woodson, *The History of the Negro Church*, 3d ed. (Associated Publishers, Inc., 1972); and Hart M. Nelsen *et al.* (eds.), *The Black Church in America* (Basic Books, Inc., 1971).

No overall history of women in American religion has been published. Such books as the following are helpful: Alice L. Hageman (ed.), *Sexist Religion and Women in the Church: No More Silence!* (Association Press, 1974); Rosemary Radford Ruether (ed.), *Religion and Sexism: Images of Women in the Jewish and Christian Traditions* (Simon & Schuster, Inc., 1974); Alice S. Rossi (ed.), *The Feminist Papers: From Adams to de Beauvoir* (Bantam Books, Inc., 1974); and Mary Daly, *The Church and the Second Sex with a New Feminist Post Christian*, rev.

ed. (Harper & Row, Publishers, Inc., 1975).

Two books are especially helpful in matters of church and state, and religious freedom in American history: Anson Phelps Stokes, *Church and State in the United States,* rev. ed. by Stokes and Leo Pfeffer (Harper & Row, Publishers, Inc., 1964), and Elwyn A. Smith, *Religious Liberty in the United States: The Development of Church-State Thought Since the Revolutionary Era* (Fortress Press, 1972).

Several recent books deal with aspects of American civil religion: Conrad Cherry (ed.), *God's New Israel: Religious Interpretations of American Destiny* (Prentice-Hall, Inc., 1971); Winthrop S. Hudson (ed.), *Nationalism and Religion in America: Concepts of American Identity and Mission* (Harper & Row, Publishers, Inc., 1970); Elwyn A. Smith (ed.), *The Religion of the Republic* (Fortress Press, 1971); Russell E. Richey and Donald G. Jones (eds.), *American Civil Religion* (Harper & Row, Publishers, Inc., 1974); Robert N. Bellah, *The Broken Covenant: American Civil Religion in Time of Trial* (The Seabury Press, Inc., 1975); and Sidney E. Mead, *The Nation with the Soul of a Church* (Harper & Row, Publishers, Inc., 1975).

Six recent books focus on aspects of American religious pluralism: Phillip E. Hammond and Benton Johnson (eds.), *American Mosaic: Social Patterns of Religion in the United States* (Random House, Inc., 1970); Robert T. Handy (ed.), *Religion in the American Experience: The Pluralistic Style* (Harper & Row, Publishers, Inc., 1972); Edwin Scott Gaustad, *Dissent in American Religion* (The University of Chicago Press, 1973); Patrick H. McNamara (ed.), *Religion American Style* (Harper & Row, Publishers, Inc., 1974); Irving I. Zaretsky and Mark P. Leone (eds.), *Religious Movements in Contemporary America* (Princeton University Press, 1974); and George Bedell, Leo Sandon, Jr., and Charles Wellborn (eds.), *Religion in America* (The Macmillan Company, 1975).

CONCLUDING HISTORIOGRAPHICAL POSTSCRIPT

One historiographical note pertains to the themes explored in this book (historiography meaning the historical development of the research, interpretation, and writing of a historical subject). The scholars of American religious history during the past half century have been preoccupied with the problem of how Christianity has been related to its social and intellectual environment. The problem has been approached from at least the following two sets of questions:

1. Has American religion developed primarily as a European transplant making its way with some adjustments and alterations in the New World but with continual instruction from the Old World? Or, has religion taken shape more in response to and as an integral part of the dynamic geographical and social-cultural American frontiers? This latter position was consistently set forth in the writings of William Warren Sweet, for example, his *Religion in the Development of American Culture, 1765–1840* (Charles Scribner's Sons, 1952). Among Sweet's more capable and appreciative critics, Winthrop S. Hudson has tended to emphasize the influence of European Christianity in American religious history, for example, his essay entitled "How American Is Religion in America?" in Jerald C. Brauer (ed.), *Reinterpretation in American Church History* (The University of Chicago Press, 1968). In recent years historians of Roman Catholicism in America have been struggling with similar problems of interpretation. Is Catholicism to be understood primarily as a variety of immigrant-ethnic churches, as a Roman-centered and therefore essentially united church, or as an Americanized and therefore distinctive (if not unique) form of Christianity quite different from European or Spanish-Mexican origins? The best analysis of this scholarly struggle is David J. O'Brien's *The Renewal of American Catholicism* (Ox-

ford University Press, 1972). Likewise students of black Christianity in America have debated over the degree to which African heritage or the American slave environment influenced the emerging black churches in America. E. Franklin Frazier, *The Negro Church in America* (Schocken Books, Inc., 1964), emphasizes the break with the African background; Henry H. Mitchell, *Black Belief: Folk Beliefs of Blacks in America and West Africa* (Harper & Row, Publishers, Inc., 1975), focuses on the continuing African influence; whereas Eugene D. Genovese, *Roll, Jordan, Roll: The World the Slaves Made* (Pantheon Books, 1974), argues for a combination of African and American influence.

2. The second set of questions is posed more broadly: To what extent does religion develop as a response to its cultural context, and to what extent does religion contain elements that influence the shaping of culture? One illustration will suffice. In 1932, Arthur M. Schlesinger, Sr., described the churches' *response* to new social and intellectual frontiers in his influential article entitled "A Critical Period in American Religion," in *Massachusetts Historical Society Proceedings,* Vol. LXIV (October 1930-June 1932), pp. 523–546. Twenty years later Robert T. Handy presented the other approach of describing "the inner drive and dynamic of the churches" in his article, "The Protestant Quest for a Christian America 1830–1930," in *Church History,* Vol. XXII (March 1952), pp. 8–20. But in my judgment the work of H. Richard Niebuhr remains unsurpassed in its analysis of the interaction of religion with the totality of American culture. His books continue to structure the problem in its many complex dimensions. The two interpretative approaches appeared in the classic studies: *The Social Sources of Denominationalism* (Henry Holt and Company, 1929) shows how Christianity has reflected its environment; and *The Kingdom of God in America* (Willett, Clark & Company, 1937) shows what

Christianity brought to its environment. Finally, Niebuhr's understanding of the complexity of how Christianity has related to its environment throughout history appeared in his great book, *Christ and Culture* (Harper & Brothers, 1951).

During the past twenty years many articles have been published at an accelerating rate on the subject of American religious historiography. Two recent essays are especially noteworthy: Edwin S. Gaustad, *Religion in America: History and Historiography* (American Historical Association, 1974), and John F. Wilson, "A Review of Some Reviews of *A Religious History of the American People,* by Sydney E. Ahlstrom," in *Religious Studies Review,* Vol. I (September 1975). One consistent objective has been to maintain or find some unifying theme in the story of American religion which does justice to the coming-of-age of religious pluralism. Altogether these historiographical essays express what might be called the scholars' quest for religious identity in America.

Index